BOMBS, TORPEDOES,

AND

KAMIKAZES

By
John W. Lambert

SPECIALTY PRESS

ISBN: 0-933424-82-5

Library of Congress Catalog Card No.: 97-91883

Text by John W. Lambert

Published by:
    Specialty Press Publishers and Wholesalers
    11481 Kost Dam Road
    North Branch, MN 55056
    Phone: 800-895-4585

Book Trade Distribution by:
    Voyageur Press
    123 North Second Street
    Stillwater, MN 55082
    Phone: 800-888-9653
    Fax: 612-430-2211

Printed in the United States of America

AIR COMBAT PHOTO HISTORY

This is the second in a series of illustrated World War II histories that graphically portray the many facets of aerial combat. Some of the rare photos are drawn from government archives and many from private collections of veterans. All show scenes of air action with captions that, as nearly as possible, identify the date, locale, and describe the event or subject. Many were taken by combat cameramen who plied their trade while the battle swirled around them.

In every case they show real battle action that occurred between 1941 and 1945, only a short step removed from the technology of World War I. These scenes will not likely be replayed in modern wars with the advent of smart bombs and long range rockets that destroy targets seen only as blips on radar screens, and missiles that enter installations over the horizon, hundreds of miles from the point of launch. World War II aerial warfare still had much of the "knights who go forth to do mortal combat" about it. The adversaries were not exactly beating on each others shields, but it was in most ways, a terrible sort of "up close and personal" warfare.

The men and aircraft are also depicted in order to give the reader a sense of the nature of the war — brave men in frail craft who went in harm's way. The deeds of warriors on both sides are viewed here so that future historians may have a record of the violent yet valiant nature of the struggle.

TABLE OF CONTENTS

INTRODUCTION

Beginning with the historic attack of December 7, 1941 on Hawaii, Japanese naval aviators exhibited skill, bravery and panache that drew grudging admiration from their opponents. However, successive engagements, culminating in the Battle of Midway, took an irretrievable toll on the most experienced Japanese air crews.

Losses were partly due to the fatalistic attitude of Japanese warriors and their willingness to die for the Emperor. It decreed that a wounded airman or one in a mortally damaged aircraft should give his life in a suicidal dive on the target. Many other Japanese, who parachuted or ditched and might have returned to fight another day, were abandoned to their fate, squandered by a higher command who were convinced of Japanese invincibility and never thought of the flyers as a limited resource. Air-sea rescue, an obsession with U.S. forces, was at best a haphazard, chance event with the Japanese.

As a consequence, the Japanese found themselves badly outmatched in the air after 1943. With their perimeter shrinking, desperation compelled a new tactic. Along with conventional attack, both Army and Navy air units sought volunteers to conduct planned suicide strikes against Allied vessels. These deadly aerial weapons were first employed by the enemy as the U.S. began the process of liberating the Philippines. They were called "Kamikaze", Japanese for Divine Wind, after the miraculous typhoon of 1281 that destroyed a Mongol invasion fleet. The Japanese hoped that invoking this image would sweep Allied naval forces from the seas. Indeed, early successes induced other Japanese aviators to utilize the new ship ramming technique. Special attack units were created to formalize the random suicide operations.

The assault of the Kamikazes did not prevent the invasion and ultimate liberation of the Philippines, but the advent of this tactic in that campaign caused incredible damage and had a sobering effect on U.S. Pacific forces. It was one thing to dodge a well delivered bomb or torpedo. Once launched they were blind weapons and the ratio of hits to misses was poor. But superlative seamanship and the most determined defense was not always adequate to prevent a tenacious pilot from crashing his aircraft onto a ship.

Toward the end of the war the Japanese Navy conceived a design that was the epitome of the suicide bomb, a rocket propelled, piloted missile called the Oka, or Cherry Blossom. U.S. forces dubbed it Baka bomb, Japanese for fool. The Yokosuka MXY7 was a flying bomb with a length of just twenty feet and a wingspan of near seventeen feet. It was designed to be carried into battle by a twin-engined bomber and released in proximity to enemy targets. Its range was a mere twenty-three miles, but once launched it could attain over 400 mph in level flight and near 600 mph in a dive. With a 1,200 pound warhead, this flying bomb was capable of having a deadly effect on even the largest naval targets. Although over 800 were built, relatively few were employed, some destroyed by AA or fighters and most failed to reach their assigned targets. Only two verifiably sunk U.S. ships, a destroyer and a landing craft.

With the subsequent invasions of Iwo Jima and Okinawa in 1945 — the Allied noose tightening to within aircraft range of the Japanese home islands — ranks of the Special Attack Units swelled. Pilots with barely twenty hours of flight training were employed in the new trade. It was reasoned that there was no need to perfect flight techniques or navigation back to base. A one-way flight and a successful dive into a ship was all that was required. Skill was gone, only bravery remained.

Allied fighter defenses extracted an incredible toll on the unpolished Kamikaze fliers. Fleet anti-aircraft fire culled more of the attackers. Still many succeeded because of their sheer numbers and perseverance.

Because of overly optimistic debriefings of a few returning attackers, Japanese commanders deluded themselves that they were causing catastrophic losses among Allied warships and transports. Thus with each Japanese defeat and Allied advance, there was bewilderment followed by resolution to fling more suicide planes at the oncoming juggernaut. The Japanese success was sufficient, however, to stun Navy commanders and cause Admiral Chester Nimitz to heavily censor any mention of the Kamikazes lest the Japanese devote more men and aircraft to the suicide missions. As the crescendo of such attacks increased, with the Okinawa campaign, there was also a concern that too much bad news about casualties caused by the Kamikazes would adversely effect morale both at the battle front and on the home front

Statistics reveal that Kamikaze aircraft sank fifty-five Allied ships, including three escort aircraft carriers, and damaged 355. Some of the damage tallies include the same ship more than once, aircraft carrier *Intrepid* CV-11, as an example, was hit by suicide planes on no less than four occasions. Some forty-six vessels were taken out of combat service as a result of battle damage.*

In this illustrated history volume we attempt to depict the relentless assault by the Japanese and the determined defense by U.S. naval forces. Courage was the order of the day for both sides in this historic struggle.

* The best sources for detailed history of Kamikaze operations are **Sacred Warriors** by Denis & Peggy Warner with Comdr. Sadao Seno, Van Norstrand Reinhold Company, 1982; **Divine Wind**, by Captain Rikihei Inoguchi and Cdr. Tadashi Nakajima with Roger Pineau, Naval Institute Press, 1958; and **History of United States Naval Operation in Worlds War II,** Vol. 12,13,14 by Samuel Eliot Morison, Atlantic Little Brown, 1960.

ACKNOWLEDGEMENTS

Many of the photos in this work are from the National Archives. However, some of the most dramatic came from individuals who preserved these rare shots for future generations. We wish to acknowledge the special assistance of John MacGlashing, Jim Lansdale, Barrett Tillman and Charles Graham.

They taught me how to fly,
   and they sent me here to die;
Where the sky is full of Zeros
   and Kamikaze heroes.
I've had a belly full of war.

Adapted from **I Wanted Wings**
a World War I song.
Origninal version by Jack Dowling

Chapter 1

THE EARLY ROUNDS

When the war began, with the Japanese attack on Hawaii – December 7, 1941 – Japan's aviators were some of the best in the world. They were highly trained and disciplined, and many of them had logged combat time in the war with China that had simmered since 1937 and in a major border clash with Russia in 1939.

They also had excellent equipment, the finest being their Mitsubishi Zero fighter, called the Zeke or Hamp (for the version with the clipped wing tips) by the Allies. In fact their naval aircraft outclassed virtually all of the U.S. Navy types in performance, except perhaps in the dive-bomber category. This advantage in aircraft quality would be quickly overcome by the Americans while the Japanese were slow to adjust and used the same types until 1945 with only limited numbers of new models.

At the start of the war the U.S. Navy had six aircraft carriers evenly split between the Atlantic and the Pacific. The Japanese had ten Pacific carriers at the start of the war, allowing her the luxury of using the six largest in the Pearl Harbor operation while much of the balance was available for operations in the South China Sea.

The leaders of the attack on Oahu were all combat veterans and, although they encountered little aerial opposition on the morning of December 7th, they executed their strike plan superbly and suffered only minimal losses: twenty-nine aircraft.

One Japanese flyer exhibited what would later become a common and terrifying tactic. Lt. Fusata Iida led the contingent of Zeros from carrier *Soryu* in an attack on Kaneohe Naval Air Station. While in the process of destroying most of the PBY Catalinas of Patrol Wing 2 that were parked on the ramp or moored in the bay, Iida was hit by ground fire. Seeing that he was loosing gasoline at a alarming rate, Iida knew that he could not make it back to his ship. So, he radioed greetings to his comrades and deliberately dove his plane into a hangar. Such acts of fatal bravado were not common in the first months of the war because the Japanese enjoyed a numerical edge over every foe they faced. That would all change with the epic Battle of Midway.

After the Pearl Harbor attack the Japanese Navy sortied boldly with carrier strikes, reaching as far west as India and as far south as Australia. Their troops swept down the Malay Peninsular and across the Dutch East Indies to the doorstep of Australia. With their meager carrier forces, the U.S. attempted to counter the enemy offense and thus the first carrier vs. carrier engagements were fought in the Coral Sea early in May 1942. Each side lost a carrier (ours was *Lexington*). Although U.S. industrial might was already laying the keels of new fleets of aircraft carriers, the balance of naval power in Spring of 1942 heavily favored the Japanese. Then came Midway where the Japanese lost four carriers to Navy bombers while the U.S. lost one, *Yorktown.* It was the turning point of the Pacific war.

A Nakajima B5N Kate rushes down the deck of Japanese aircraft carrier *Akagi* for the Pearl Harbor attack. Her deadly torpedo, seen slung below the belly, weighed 1,764 lbs. (NARS)

Japanese aircraft carrier *Shokaku* prepares to launch her aircraft for the second wave attack on Oahu. Foreground is a Mitsubishi A6M-2B Zero (Zeke in Allied parlance) that will fly CAP, and behind it are a squadron of Nakajima B5N Kate bombers. (NARS)

Aichi Val D3A dive-bombers (above) were the work horses of the Japanese naval air arm, being used throughout the war from both aircraft carriers and land bases. It generally carried a 550 lb. bomb (seen here) under the belly and mounted two fixed .303 machine guns in the nose and a single flexible .303 caliber in the rear cockpit. This Val is from the 582nd Kokutai stationed at Bougainville in the Solomons in 1942. (Lambert)

Lt. Zenji Abe, (right) who flew an Aichi Val dive-bomber in the second Pearl Harbor attack wave, can be seen here posing before a Zero fighters on board the carrier *Akagi* just before the attack. He was one of the rare experienced Japanese naval aviators to survive the war. (Z. Abe)

7 Dec 1941. A photo of Ford Island, Pearl Harbor looking northeast, taken by the Japanese. A Val dive-bomber can be seen (center) pulling out of her attack and flying over battleship row early in the raid. A pillar of water and smoke, likely from a torpedo, can be seen rising from one of the battleships to the left of the Val. The battleships (left to right) are: *Nevada, Arizona* with repair ship *Vestal* alongside; *Tennessee* (inside) and *West Virginia, Maryland,* and *Oklahoma* (where the plume of water is rising); oiler *Neosho* (under the Val); and *California*. (NARS)

Battleship *California* BB-44, took torpedo hits along her port side and settled into the mud of Pearl Harbor. Then a bomb penetrated touching off her AA ammunition magazine. Fires on the water from ships astern of her added to the problem, forcing the crew to abandon ship. Ninety-eight of her crew were killed and 61 injured. Refloated over three months later, *California* had to be repaired in Bremerton and did not rejoin the fleet until mid-1944. (NARS)

A Japanese Val dive bomber, is hit by ship's AA fire over Pearl Harbor and plunges. A total of 29 Japanese aircraft were lost in the raid on Oahu, their dive bombers suffering the heaviest losses. (NARS)

Gallant battleship *Nevada*, despite the absence of her captain and many crew members, got underway during the attack, commanded by Lt. Lawrence E. Ruff. She had left battleship row and was approaching the Pearl Harbor channel when the Japanese strike leader, Lt. Cdr. Mitsuo Fuchida, directed an incoming strike from *Kaga* at the huge target. They scored several hits on the stern half of the ship starting fires and causing concern that she might sink, blocking the channel. Assisted by tugs (one of which is in foreground), *Nevada* was beached at Waipio Point where her fires were extinguished. She lost 50 killed and 109 wounded. *Nevada* was refloated two months later and rejoined the fleet in 1943 after extensive repairs and refitting. (NARS)

Battleship *Pennsylvania* BB-38 had no chance to sortie as did *Nevada. Pennsylvania* was trapped in the permanent dry dock at the Navy Yard. Ahead of her were destroyers *Downes* DD-375 (left) and *Cassin* DD-372 (right). The crews of all three manned their guns and fought back, but this huge stationary target was an irresistible target for both Japanese Vals and Kates. The dry dock was flooded to help reduce the fire potential, but *Cassin* rolled off her blocks sustaining ever greater damage. The two destroyers had to be virtually rebuilt, but *Pennsylvania* sustained relatively little damage. (NARS)

(Above): The Japanese employed some 350 aircraft, from six carriers, in two waves for the attack on Pearl Harbor, concentrating primarily on the fleet anchorage and secondarily on airfields. Here a Kate torpedo bomber from *Kaga,* piloted by Lt. Minori Suzuki is lifted from the bottom of Southeast Loch, where it fell to ship's AA fire after delivering its torpedo. (NARS)

(Right): This Mitsubishi Zero (Zeke to the Allies) from carrier *Akagi* was in the first wave attack. It crashed near Ft. Kam on Oahu. Its pilot was Petty Officer Takashi Hirano. The Japanese lost just nine aircraft from the first wave, but twenty from the second. (NARS)

16

After raiding Wake Island on 20 Feb 42, the *Lexington* task force came under attack from Japanese Mitsubishi Betty's based in the Marshalls. Lt. Butch O'Hare distinguished himself (and won a Medal of Honor) by downing five enemy planes. One, pictured here with right engine smoking, the disabled aircraft of Lt. Cdr. Takuzo Ito, attempted unsuccessfully to crash into "Lady Lex". This was one of the earliest examples of a Japanese pilot willing to spend his life in a suicide attempt. (NARS)

Japanese carrier air groups from *Shokaku* and *Zuikaku* struck Task Force 17 on 8 May 42 in the Coral Sea will considerable skill, sinking *Lexington* and damaging *Yorktown*. Here a Kate bursts into flames during her torpedo attack. (NARS)

8 May 1942. the Battle of the Coral Sea was the first in history between carriers. Torpedo planes and dive bombers from *Shokaku* and *Zuikaku* attacked simultaneously. Above: The *Lexington* CV-2 is taking hits as she attempts to avoid torpedo carrying Kates, one of which can be seen approaching her port bow. She dodged nearly a dozen torpedoes but was hit by a pair and then by two bombs and took two near misses that ruptured plates. Below: Her crew fought for several hours to save her, but uncontrollable fires defeated them. Shortly after "Abandon Ship" had been ordered (note life rafts off the bow) an explosion racked Lady Lex and she sank. (NARS)

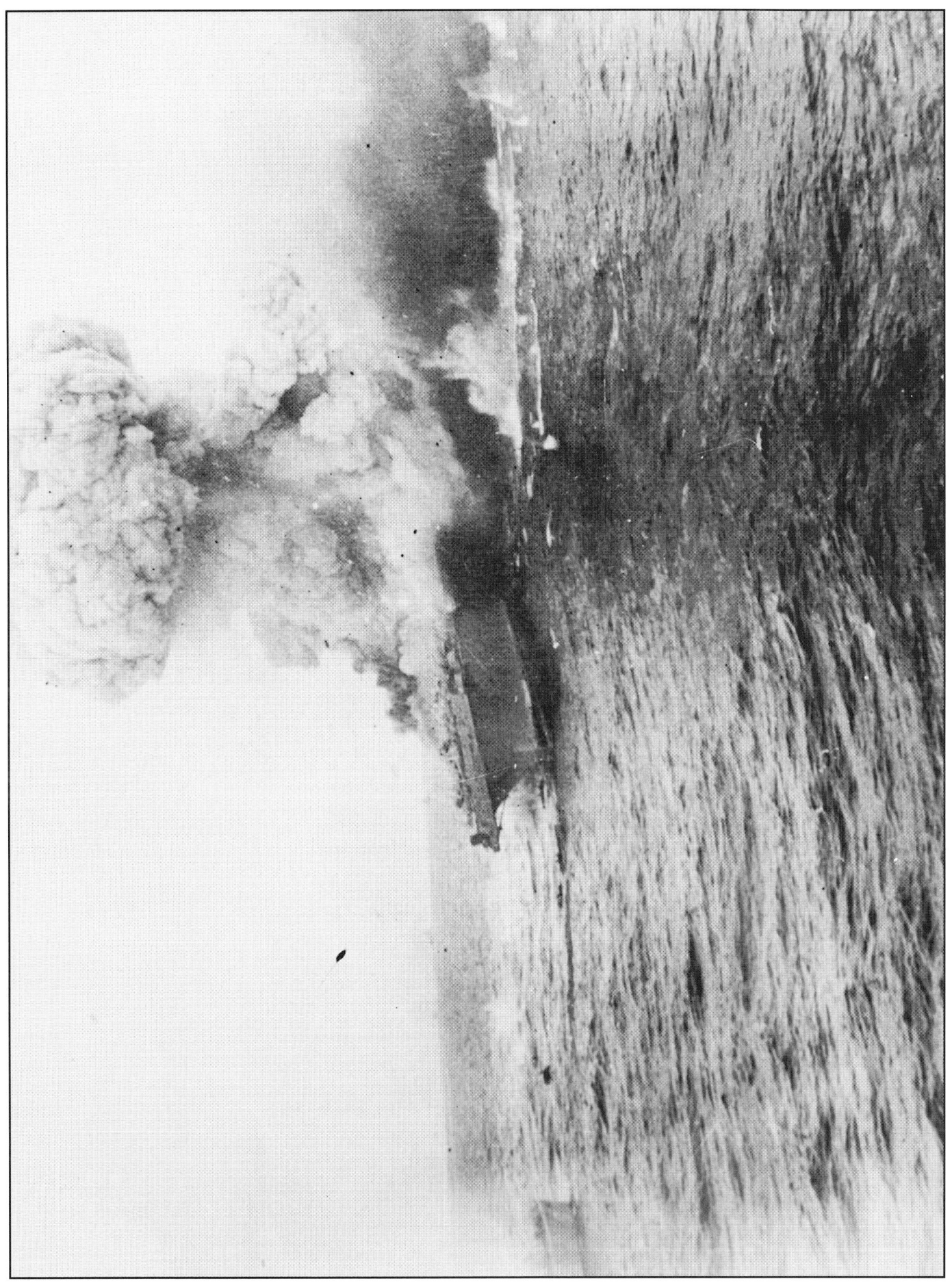

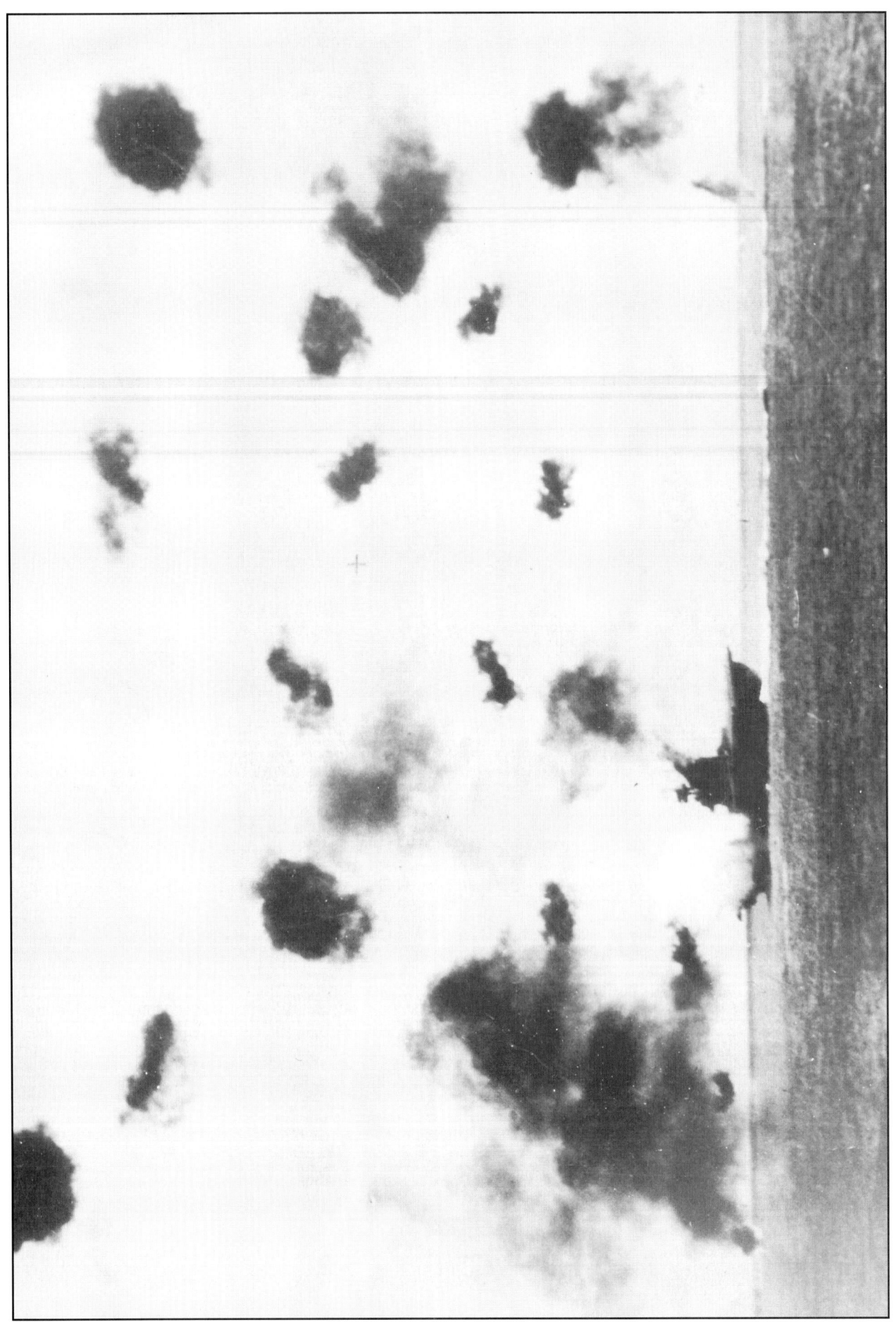

Yorktown CV-5 under attack on 4 Jun 1942 (above) by aircraft from *Hiryu* during the epic Battle of Midway. Although battered by bombs and torpedoes, her crew fought valiantly to save the listing carrier (below), but were forced to abandon ship. Still *Yorktown* refused to sink and escorts hovered about until 7 Jun when Japanese submarine I-168 fired a spread of torpedoes that sank both *Yorktown* and one of the escorting destroyers, *Hammann*. *(NARS)*

In the Battle of the Santa Cruz Islands, 26-27 Oct 1942, a Japanese Kate (above) approaches the carrier *Hornet* CV-8 through a flak speckled sky. The Japanese pilot has dropped his torpedo (below), obtaining a strike near the stern of *Hornet*, then escapes flying past the carrier. (USN)

In a marvelously coordinated attack a Val dive-bomber plummets from above *Hornet as* the Kate (from preceding page) is still seen retreating. The Val pilot was dead or dying, but his aim was true. He struck aft of the stack near the signal bridge and sheared off onto the deck (below). The Japanese aircraft in this strike came from *Shokaku* and *Zuikaku*. (USN)

Left: A view of the signal bridge where the Val first struck. (NARS)

The carnage caused by the crashing Val, can be sensed in this smoke shrouded scene (below). Japanese carrier planes attacked and hit *Hornet* three more times, *Zuiho* and *Junyo*'s air groups joining the battle. Dead in the water, a 14 degree list to starboard and internal fires that could not be controlled compelled the crew to abandon ship late on 26 Oct. As the U.S. fleet withdrew a destroyer fired many torpedoes into *Hornet*. Burning furiously she still refused to sink until a Japanese flotilla approached and finished her in the darkness. (NARS)

It is August 1942 and U.S. forces are hanging on by a thread at Guadalcanal. The Japanese Navy and their air units made unremitting efforts to dislodge the American beachhead in the Solomon Islands. Here a flight of Mitsubishi G4M Bettys from Rabaul, some of the few who had escaped the CAP of Wildcats from *Saratoga* and *Enterprise* and fleet AA fire, conduct a torpedo attack on discharging transports on 8 Aug. Their only success was the sinking of destroyer *Jarvis* DD-393. (USMC)

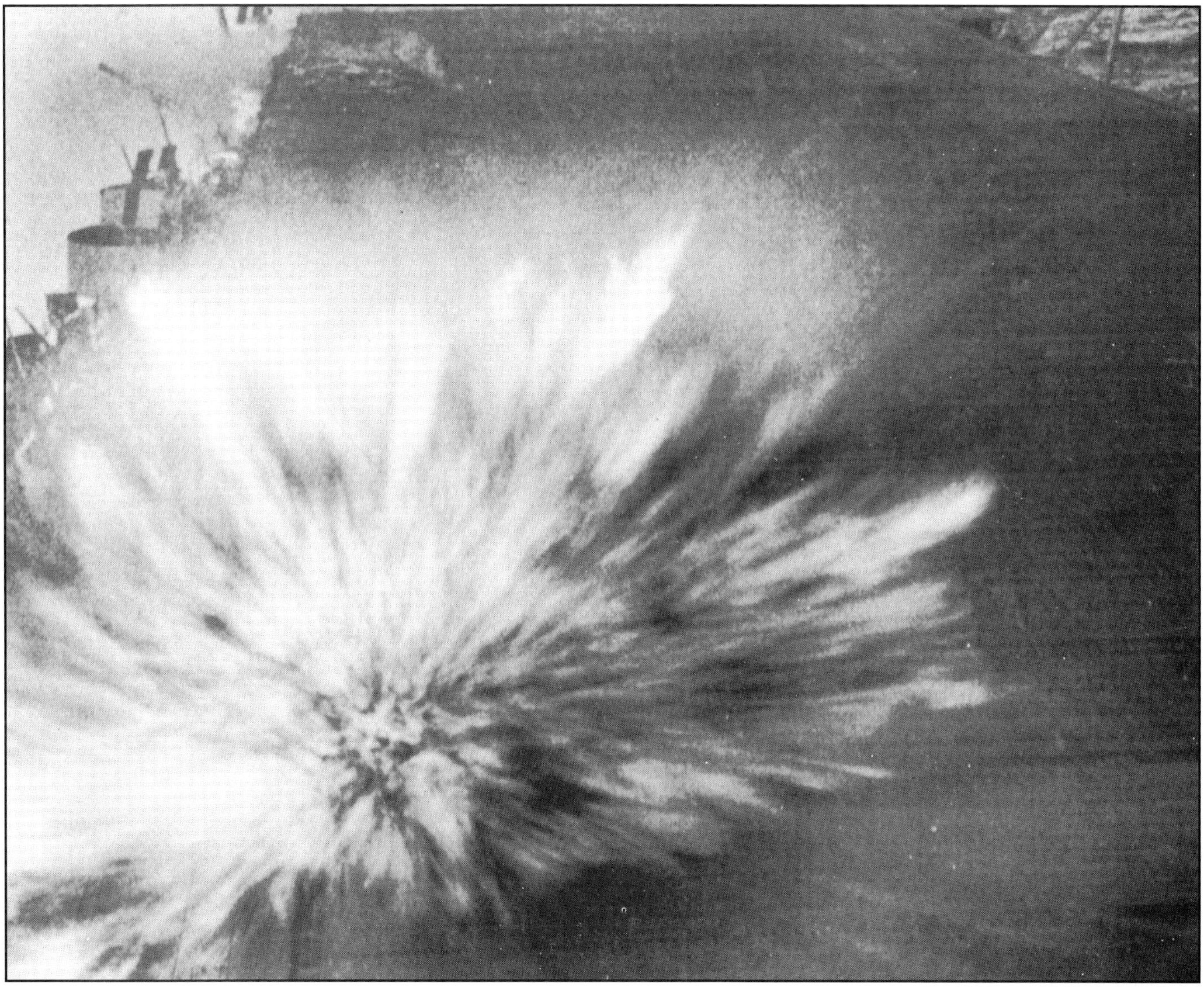

On the afternoon of 24 August 1942 during the Battle of the Eastern Solomons, an aircraft carrier slugging match, *Enterprise* CV-6 took three bomb hits, from dozens that were aimed at her, when attacked by Vals of *Shokaku, Zuikaku* and *Ryujo.* Thanks to gallant efforts by her crew, the *Enterprise* survived, but 75 sailors were killed and 95 wounded in the attack. Photographers Mate Robert F. Read calmly shot pictures of the attack, including this one of the explosion of a bomb near the starboard aft 5 inch turret. His incredible photo survived but he died. (NARS)

Chapter 2

PIERCING JAPAN'S OUTER DEFENSE

Late 1942 victories for the Allies at Guadalcanal and on the lower tip of New Guinea, reversed the southern drive of the Japanese Army. Gaining strength, the Allies then began the long road back via 1943 invasions of the Gilbert and then the Marshall Islands.

To secure these victories growing U.S. carrier task forces began to batter the Carolines, and the island strongholds of the Bismarck Archipelago. Then, in a bold leapfrogging move, the Allies bypassed many Japanese island bases to invade the Marianas Islands in the Central Pacific in mid-1944.

The naval battles associated with these campaigns, scattered over a vast area of ocean 2,000 miles in each direction, were fought largely by aircraft against ships, the Japanese utilizing both land and sea based aviation. U.S. Navy aircraft carriers became the focal point of Japanese attacks. For it was the dominance of air power that determined the winners in the island hopping war.

One of these campaigns, the Marianas, brought out the Japanese fleet carriers. But the losses suffered at Coral Sea and Midway, and the aerial battles of attrition in New Guinea, the Solomons and at Rabaul had already robbed the Japanese of too many experienced air crews. The great carrier duel fought out west of the Marianas in the Philippine Sea was the largest of such engagements.

Attacking the U.S. fleet with unbridled fury the Japanese squandered an estimated 407 aircraft (both land and carrier based) while destroying not a single U.S. carrier. It became known as the Marianas Turkey Shoot. American losses were 97 carrier aircraft, many of their crews being rescued. In the second round pursuit of the Japanese fleet, U.S. aircraft and submarines sank three carriers, five destroyers and two fleet oilers. But the greatest toll for the Japanese was the further loss of quality naval air crews. They could no longer send squadrons of highly trained, battle tested airmen into battle. They could still build replacement aircraft but were running out of experience in the cockpit. This lack of expertise forced the Japanese to resort to a desperation tactic — suicide attacks.

A Nakajima B5N Kate. This one was captured and brought to the U.S. for flight testing and evaluation. In the early rounds of the war these torpedo carrying aircraft did great damage to the Navy. (NARS)

The Mitsubishi A6M Zero fighter (Zeke or Hamp to the Allies) had the advantage at the beginning of World War II, but by 1944 it was inferior to the latest Allied fighters. This particular aircraft was found intact in Japan after the 1945 surrender. (Lambert)

More Mitsubishi G4M "Bettys" were produced than any other Japanese bomber. Employed in both conventional and torpedo roles by the Navy, it had great load capacity and range but no protection for the fuel tanks, making it highly vulnerable. This photo of a -2 was taken at Clark Field in 1945. The ship seems undamaged. (USAF via Jim Lansdale)

The Yokosuka D4Y (named Judy by the Allies) was the Japanese replacement for the aging Aichi Val dive bomber. It first saw limited service in reconnaissance at the Battle of Midway, but by the time it appeared in any numbers most of Japan's aircraft carriers had been sunk and skilled aircrews lost. Still, operating mostly from island bases they were used effectively in both the attack and suicide roles. Its maximum speed was near 360 mph compared to the old Val's 280. (Jim Lansdale)

The April 29-30, 1944 attack of Task Force 58 on the Japanese bastion of Truk elicited a furious response. A Nakajima B6N, Jill torpedo bomber, her deadly fish visible, pursued the aircraft carrier, *Hornet* CV-10, through a torrent of anti-aircraft fire, as shown in this sequence. The pilot may have been mortally wounded and unable to release his torpedo as the Jill plunged into the water astern of *Hornet* still carrying her "fish". While smaller caliber guns fired directly at an oncoming attacker, the bigger batteries of warships fired ahead, hoping that the geyser of water might down a low flying enemy aircraft. (NARS)

A Yokosuka D4Y Judy is set afire by U.S. Navy flak batteries during an attempted low level attack on 19 Jun 1944 during the first Battle of the Philippine Sea. It crashed harmlessly into the ocean. (Barrett Tillman)

The failure of the Japanese to mount successful conventional attacks, because of the earlier loss of veteran air crews, is exhibited in this scene. It was 23 Jun 44 off the Marianas. The escort carrier *Manila Bay* CVE-61 was delivering AAF 318th Fighter Grp P-47s to Saipan and was hooked to a fleet oiler. On the other side of the oiler was an escorting battleship. Suddenly four Japanese Vals were detected overhead and began their bomb runs. As all hands went to battle stations, lines between ships were cut and hoses disconnected, spraying fuel oil in all directions, and ships went to flank speed. Despite the closely bunched targets, all four bombs missed astern, three visible here raising waterspouts. One Val can just be seen climbing away. (USN)

The scene is the South China Sea off Formosa on 14 Oct 1944, where TF 38 attacked Japanese airfields in support of the pending Leyte invasion. The white streaks and dots are tracer rounds from light AA cannon on carrier *Lexington* CV-16. Those deadly streaks, one tracer round out of every five, give a sense of the blizzard of lead that could be thrown up by just one ship. There is a Japanese bomber out there somewhere, low on the water, and he did not score. (NARS)

Chapter 3

LIBERATION OF THE PHILIPPINES

With the Allied invasion armada massed off Leyte and Samar, the Japanese unleashed the Divine Wind on 25 Oct 1944. Eight U.S. Navy aircraft carriers were hit by air attack in the first day, seven by suicide crashes.

In less than three months of naval operations during the Philippine campaign, approximately 140 Allied ships were hit by Kamikaze attacks. This does not count conventional air attacks nor the naval engagement precipitated by the sortie of the Japanese fleet known as the Battle of Leyte Gulf.

The Philippine campaign involved both conventional and suicide attacks by the Japanese. Both were effective, but continuing losses of men and aircraft convinced the Japanese that the suicide attack was easier for less qualified airmen than the skill required for a torpedo run or dive-bombing a moving warship. And the longer the conflict lasted the thinner became the ranks of highly proficient veterans.

U.S. ground forces also found tough going in the liberation of the Philippines, making the entire campaign — air, sea and ground — one of heavy losses on both sides. America had the wherewithal to replace their skilled casualties, but the Japanese reliance on Kamikaze attacks was a slippery slope from which there was no retreat. The success of the suicide pilots simply called for more sacrifice in an endless chain of fanaticism and death. A chain that could only be broken by the surrender of Japanese armed forces. At the start of 1945 that seemed a long way off, and Allied sailors who had witnessed Kamikaze attacks were understandably terrified at the prospect of having to face such fanatics in successive campaigns.

Right: Capt. Sakae Yamamoto of the 201st Kokutai (on crutch due to an injury from a crash landing), addresses the first Japanese pilots to be dispatched on suicide missions. The date was 25 Oct 1944 and the place was Mabalacat, P.I. (James Zyduck via James Lansdale)

Below: The Yokosuka P1Y1 was one of Japan's most attractive and best performing bombers of WW II. Dubbed "Frances" by the Allies, late models of this Navy aircraft had a max. speed of over 360 mph. It was utilized in many Kamikaze attacks late in the war, starting with the Philippines. This aircraft bears the markings of the Yokosuka Kokutai. (Don Thorpe via Jim Lansdale)

Early on the morning of 24 Oct 1944 the Japanese began attacking the Leyte invasion armada. Many enemy aircraft were downed by ships batteries and fighter protection, but a single Japanese bomber pilot in a Yokosuka D4A Judy, filtered through the defenses and, with superb skill, dropped a single 550 lbs. bomb amidships on carrier *Princeton.* The bomb passed through three decks, igniting gasoline storage that eventually set off Avengers spotted on her stern. Cruiser *Reno* stands by to render assistance. (NARS)

With their doomed ship, *Princeton,* burning in the background, aircraft from Air Group 27 sought refuge aboard on any flight deck that was available. Here a VF-27 Grumman F6F Hellcat lands aboard *Essex.* (Charles Graham)

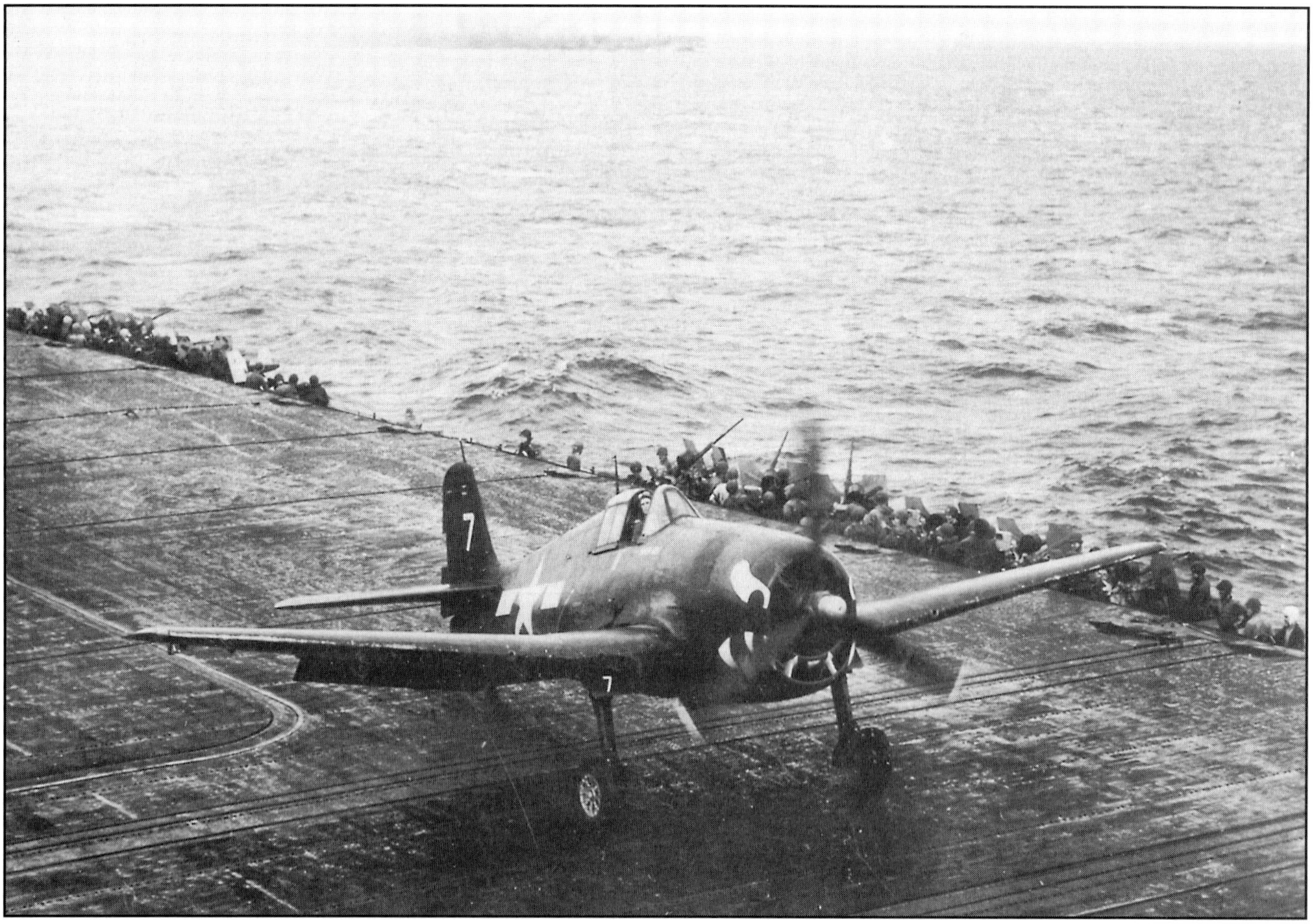

Above: *Princeton*'s crew fought the fires to a near standstill. This close view from cruiser *Birmingham* shows the carnage on *Princeton*'s aft flight deck and an elevator blown down to the hangar deck. She was adrift at this point. (Barrett Tillman)
Below: Suddenly, in mid-afternoon with cruiser *Birmingham* close by the carrier's port side, a tremendous magazine explosion ripped off *Princeton's* fantail and she eventually sank. *Birmingham*, her decks filled with fire fighters, gunners and men preparing to pass lines for a towing operation, was raked with shrapnel. The loss of life on both ships was terrible, 351 killed or missing and 552 wounded from *Princeton* and 234 killed or missing and 408 wounded from *Birmingham*, all as a result of one well placed bomb. (NARS)

Santee CVE-29 (left) was the first Kamikaze victim. This is the instant that a Zero crashed her port side near the flight deck. The relatively small bomb carried by the Japanese plane detonated on the hangar deck. The aft end of *Santee* can be seen (below) just minutes after the event, with wreckage and smoke billowing from a hangar deck fire. She suffered 16 killed and 27 wounded. (NARS)

Suwanee CVE-27 was next to be hit. She appears dead in the water (above) but is backing to keep the bow fire from reaching fueled and armed planes on her deck. After the fires are extinguished (below) *Suwanee's* crew work to repair her flight deck. (NARS)

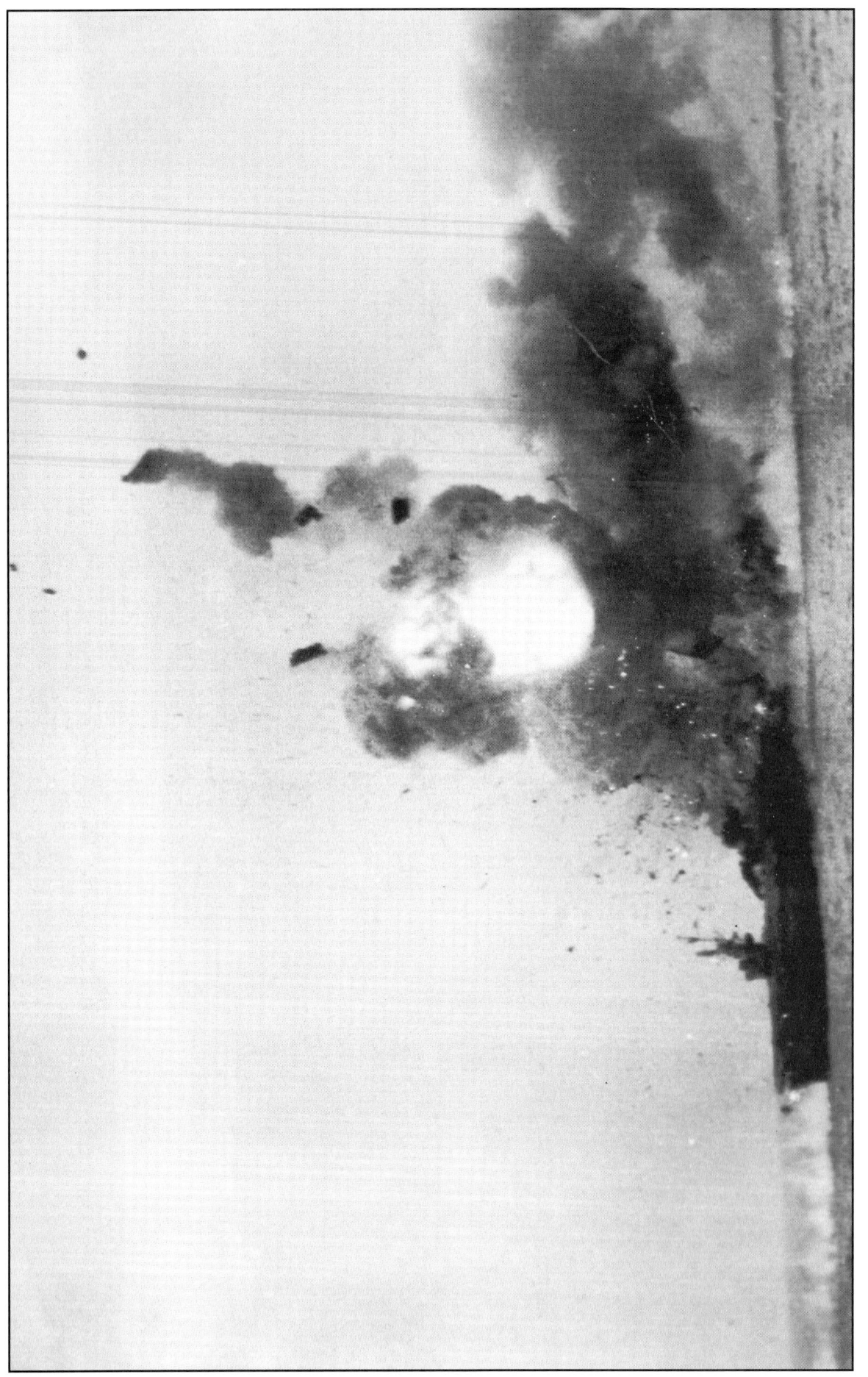

At mid-morning on 25 Oct 1944 *St. Lo* CVE-63 observed a Zeke approaching from her stern in a shallow dive as if on a landing approach. The Japanese pilot, believed to be Lt. Yukio Seki, took no evasive action, leading a seemingly charmed life, despite frantic AA from *St. Lo* and other ships. He swept across the stern of the carrier, her decks filled with six aircraft some loading torpedoes, dropped his bomb, rolled over and crashed. The Zero's momentum carried it along the flight deck as its bomb penetrated the hangar deck and exploded (above). After a series of eight internal explosions, *St. Lo* was abandoned and sank. That one Zero and one bomb that sank the carrier had also taken 114 lives and wounded scores. It was the first confirmed sinking for a Kamikaze pilot.

A Japanese Frances is flamed above the Leyte invasion fleet late on 25 Oct 1944 and plunges toward the ocean, crashing very near *Kitkun Bay* CVE-71. Gruman Avengers, wings folded, are seen on the deck of another escort carrier. (NARS)

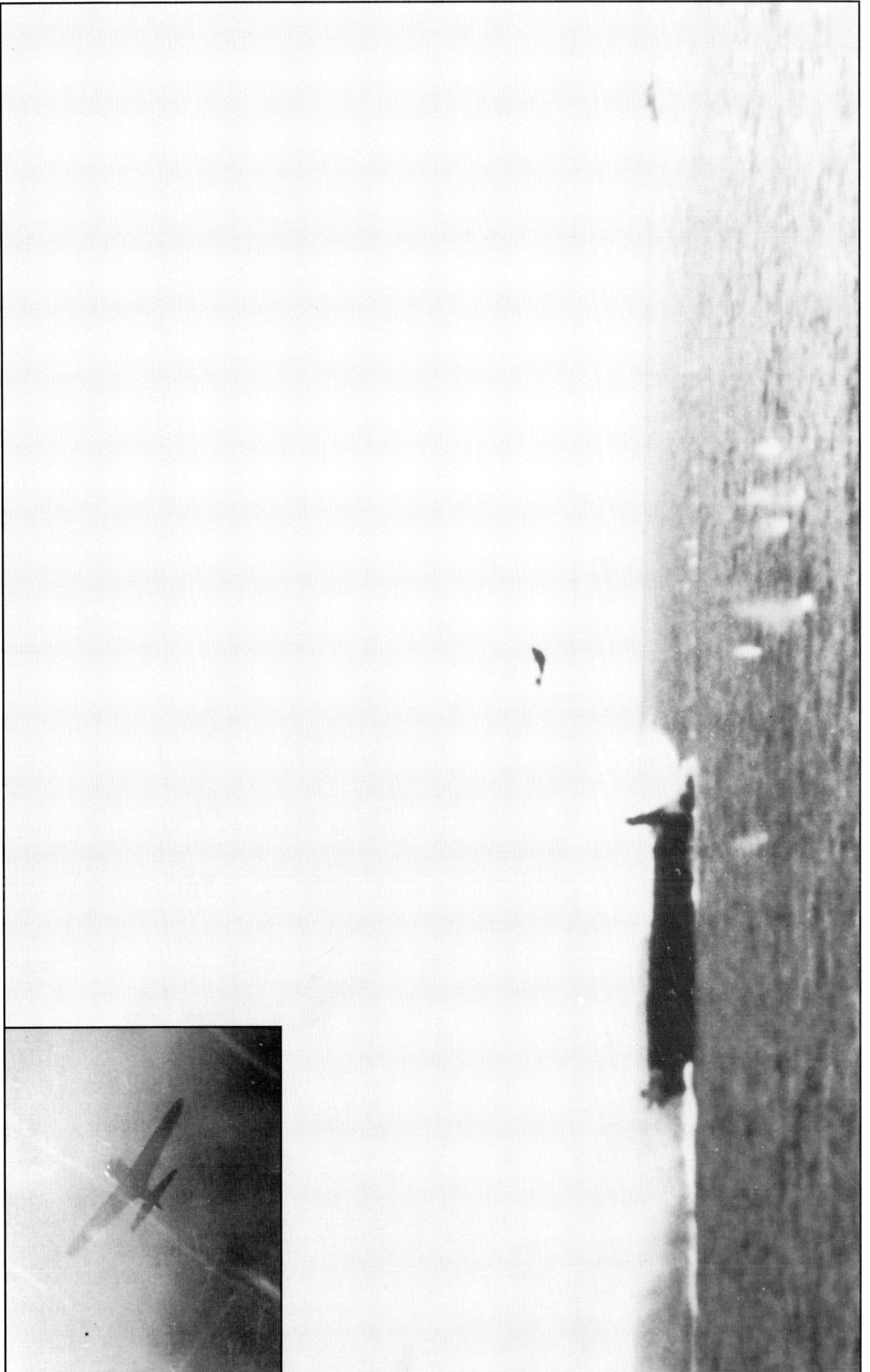

Suwanee CVE-27 was attacked and hit on both Oct 25 and 26th off Leyte. On the preceding page, she is shown under way on 26 Oct 44 with a Zeke from a Cebu based Japanese unit diving toward her. The Japanese pilot crashed the flight deck (below) hitting squarely on an Avenger that had just landed and was spotted on the forward elevator. Following directly behind the first Zeke, a second one just visible off the starboard bow dropped a bomb that plunged through the flight deck and added to the carnage. A Grumman from *Suwanee's* Air Group 60 flies past during the attack. The *Suwanee* was saved by the gallant efforts of her crew, but over 140 of her crew were killed, including the captain, and over 100 injured. One of the attackers is captured in the inset photo. (NARS)

Sangamon CVE-26 took a near miss by a Kamikaze sustaining slight damage. She is shown here under attack with her starboard aft 20mm guns spewing smoke as they throw up a curtain of flak. (NARS)

The sky was full of Zeros and Hellcats above *Belleau Wood* CVL-24 on 30 Oct 1944 off Samar. A Japanese fighter dives toward the carrier (above) as two Hellcats returning from a Manila strike overfly the scene. The carrier was seriously damaged (below) losing 92 of her crew killed and 54 seriously injured. Twelve planes were destroyed by fire, and *Belleau Wood* was forced to withdraw from the battle to Ulithi for extensive repairs. (NARS)

On 1 Nov 1944 a Japanese Francis twin-engine bomber made a run at *Ammen* DD-527. Disabled by flak the enemy aircraft sheered off the destroyer's midship's superstructure and crashed alongside. (NARS)

Japanese attackers swarmed about the Leyte invasion fleet on 1 Nov 44 concentrating on five destroyers, sinking one and causing serious damage to four others despite a furious AA defense by the DDs and other ships and the CAP. A determined Val dove on *Abner Read* DD-526, lost a wing to flak but still managed to stay on course. Its bomb went down the stack into the boiler room and the fuselage of the plane crashed just aft the stack setting off torpedoes and starting fires. This is the view a few minutes later after an enormous explosion racked the ship breaking her virtually in half. As rescue efforts by destroyers *Leary* and *Claxton* are underway another Val was shot down nearby (the white plume). Incredibly, *Abner Read* lost only 22 of her crew. (NARS)

In the Philippine sea East of Luzon on 5 Nov 44, Task Force 38 was assaulted by numerous Japanese aircraft. The CAP downed many, but four Zekes eluded the protecting fighters. Three were downed by flak, but one (seen just before impact) dove into *Lexington* CV-16, crashing on the starboard side of her aft island structure. Damage control efforts were courageous and the *Lexington* resumed flight operations within 20 minutes. But she had suffered the loss of 50 and injury to 132 of her crew. (NARS)

On 5 Nov 1944 a mortally wounded Japanese attacker flies perilously across carrier *Ticonderoga* CV-14, deck packed with airplanes (above), and crashes to the sea in yet another gallant but futile gesture (below). (NARS)

Aircraft carrier *Intrepid* CV-11 came under attack in the waters off Luzon on 25 Nov 1944 and was hit by two Kamikazes. A Japanese Judy can be seen (above) as if on a base leg aft of *Intrepid.* It turns toward the carrier (below) and is hit by flak, emitting a streamer of smoke, but continues in its run, striking a 20mm gun mount that fired until its crew was killed. The Judy's bomb penetrated to a lower deck before exploding. (NARS) See following page.

Minutes after suffering the first suicide attack, the fires aboard *Intrepid* attracted another Kamikaze. It struck aft penetrating to the hangar deck. In all 69 men were killed and 44 wounded. *Intrepid's* crew battled the fires and saved the ship. (NARS)

The Japanese Judy dive bomber seconds before striking the flight deck of *Essex* CV-9 on 25 Nov 1944. See following pages for other photos of this incident. (USN)

Above: The crash of the Judy on Essex looks worse than it was at the instant of the hit. Actually the attacker struck the port side of the flight deck a glancing blow. When the fires (below) were extinguished, *Essex* buried their 15 dead ar sea. After the 25 Nov 1944 Kamikaze strikes on *Intrepid, Essex and Cabot* Admiral Halsey withdrew his fast carriers from within range of Japanese airfields on Luzon. (NARS)

Cruiser *St. Louis* CL-49 can be seen (above) through the rigging of another ship on 27 Nov 1944 as she throws up flak while having just sustained the crash of a Kamikaze on her stern turrets. A second suicide aircraft dives upside down on her. It crashed off the starboard stern quarter. *St. Louis* survived, but with her after turrets out of commission and catapults and float planes destroyed she limped away to Manus Is. for repairs. (NARS)

Near dusk on 29 Nov 1944 battleship *Maryland* BB-46 was cruising in Leyte Gulf. A lone Japanese Army Nakajima Ki-43, Oscar dove on her with little warning from overcast skies and rain squalls. Apparently deciding that his alignment was bad, the Japanese pilot pulled back up into the cloud cover and dove again, almost vertically, seemingly immune to ships' anti-aircraft fire. The Oscar struck between the two forward turrets, killing 31 and wounding 30. A photographer on battleship *New Mexico* recorded the moment of impact. (NARS)

With the ground battle for Leyte Island entering its seventh week of grim jungle warfare, Gen. MacArthur invaded the west side of Leyte at Ormoc Bay on 7 Dec 1944. *Ward* APD-16 carried part of the dawn landing force to the beach. *Ward* had been one of the heroes of the Pearl Harbor attack just three years before, sinking a Japanese midget sub at the entrance to Pearl Harbor. Japanese aircraft attacked in strength, and despite heavy anti-aircraft fire and a cap of P-38 fighters overhead, three enemy bombers went after *Ward* like avenging angels. Two crashed nearby but one, on fire, crashed amidships, its engine penetrating into the boiler room. *Ward's* crew was rescued by other ships, then the mortally wounded veteran was finally sunk by gunfire from *O'Brien* DD-725 whose skipper, Cdr. William Outerbridge, had been CO of *Ward* on 7 Dec 1941. (NARS)

52

The sequence on this page and the next show a Japanese Frances approaching *Ommaney Bay* CVE-79 on 15 Dec 1944, intent on a suicide attack.(right) (NARS)

Aflame and with a dead pilot probably at the controls, it flies just over the stern of *Ommaney Bay* (below). (NARS)

53

Left: Mortally crippled the Frances rolls into a death dive as a 20mm gun crew of the *Omanney Bay* (foreground) continues to fire. (NARS)

Below: The Japanese Kamikaze crashes into the sea off the carrier's starboard side (below). (NARS)

As the Allied Luzon invasion force of some 160 vessels proceeded through the Sulu Sea on 4 Jan 1945. *Ommaney Bay*'s luck ran out. A lone D4Y Judy dive-bomber approached the fleet near dusk, undetected by radar. The Japanese pilot singled out the escort carrier (above), dove on her and crashed midships on the flight deck loaded with parked aircraft. One of the Judy's 250 kilogram bombs penetrated the deck and exploded in the hangar. Another penetrated to the second platform deck before detonating. With water lines severed, fires raged as bombs and torpedoes on parked aircraft began exploding, raining debris on destroyers that had come close to assist. Within one hour the surviving crew members were abandoning ship from bow and stern. Losses were 93 killed or missing and 65 wounded. Again it was another stunning success for the beleaguered Japanese, confirming their faith in suicide tactics. (NARS)

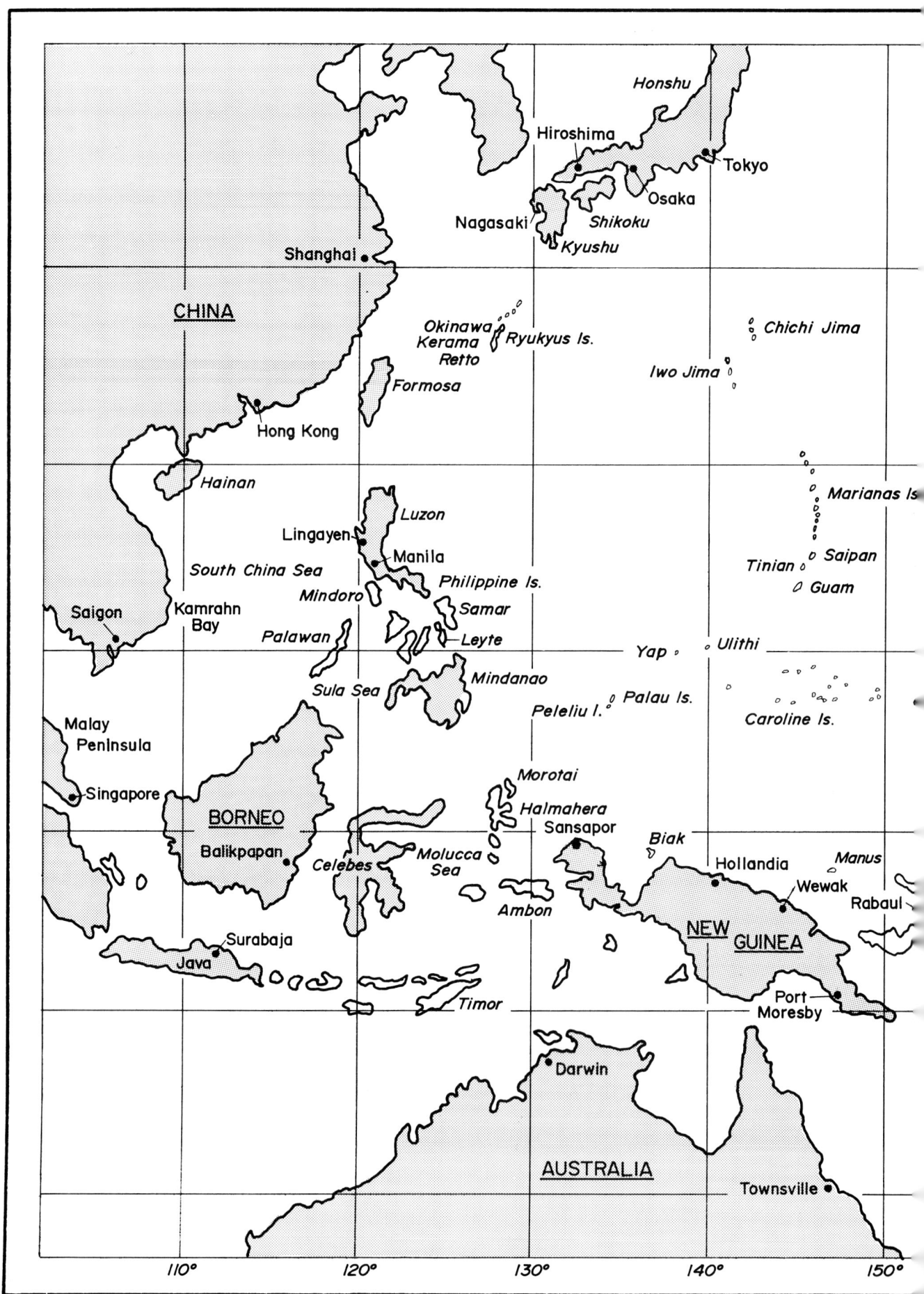

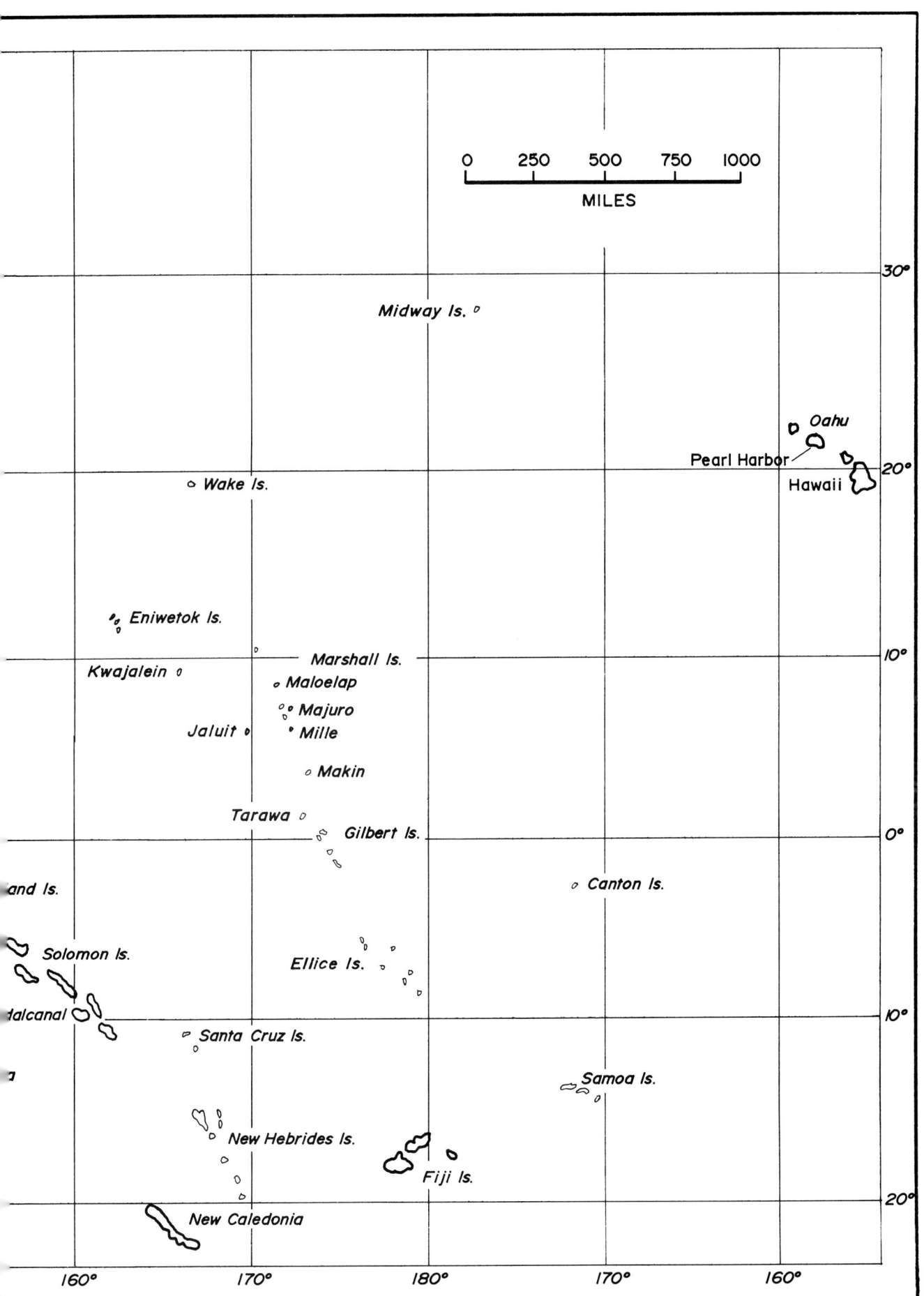

0   250   500   750   1000

MILES

30°

Midway Is. ⬭

Oahu
Pearl Harbor
Hawaii   20°

⬭ Wake Is.

⬭ Eniwetok Is.

10°

Marshall Is. ⬭

Kwajalein ⬭   ⬭ Maloelap

⬭⬭ Majuro

Jaluit ⬭   • Mille

⬭ Makin

Tarawa ⬭   Gilbert Is.

0°

⬭ Canton Is.

...and Is.

Solomon Is.   Ellice Is.

...dalcanal

10°

⬭ Santa Cruz Is.

Samoa Is.

New Hebrides Is.

Fiji Is.

20°

New Caledonia

160°   170°   180°   170°   160°

The approach of the invasion fleet to Lingayen on 6 Jan 1945 provoked a hornets nest of Japanese Navy Kamikazes. Twelve Allied warships were hit and several more suffered from near misses. A Zeke (inset) begins to disintegrate from AA fire as it closes with *New Mexico* BB-40. (NARS)

Above: The moment of impact when the Zeke strikes *New Mexico* forward of amidships, killing her captain and many others. (NARS)

A wrecked gun mount (above) on *New Mexico*, and the port wing of the navigation bridge (below) attest to the death and destruction. There were 31 killed and 87 wounded, but *New Mexico* stayed on station. Among those killed on the port bridge wing were Time correspondent William Chickering, Lt. Gen. Herbert Lumsden, an observer from Winston Churchill's staff, and the ship's CO, Capt. R.W. Fleming. (NARS)

Off Lingayen Gulf, a Japanese Kamikaze (above) dove through the combined fire of heavy cruiser *Louisville* CL-28 (on the far left) and her escorting destroyers and crashed, striking on the starboard side abreast the bridge structure (following page). She had been hit earlier in the day and her captain seriously injured. *Louisville* lost 32 killed and 56 wounded on 6 Jan 1945. *Louisville* was one of 14 Allied ships to be hit by suicide attackers on this day. (NARS)

Above: Cruiser *Columbia* CL-56 was narrowly missed by a Kamikaze, that passed between her masts off Lingayen Gulf. A few hours later a second Japanese suicide plane dove through the flak (a Zeke with hydraulics gone and the landing gear extended) and executed a perfect crash on the main deck with such tremendous force that parts of the plane and its bomb penetrated two more decks before detonating. The explosion (following page) makes it seem extraordinary that *Columbia* could survive. But survive she did, getting her fires under control and continuing on station despite the loss of 13 killed and 44 wounded. (NARS)

Chapter 4

THE FINAL BLOODY STRUGGLE

All of the desperate island campaigns from Guadalcanal through the Marianas were preludes to the invasion of what the Japanese considered their sacred territory on the doorstep of the Home Islands. The landings on Iwo Jima, 650 miles from Honshu, and Okinawa, just 330 miles from Kyushu, were resisted with even greater fanaticism than the previous encroachments.

Battleships, aircraft carriers and transports were priority targets for the Japanese. And the bigger the target, the easier it was to hit with bomb, torpedo or Kamikaze. But the Japanese gave nearly equal attention to the small ships; landing craft, mine sweepers, destroyers and destroyer escorts. Many of the DDs were stationed at a distance of 40 to 90 miles from Okinawa as pickets to provide early warning of impending attacks. It was often lonely duty, with no fleet to provide a mantle of anti-aircraft fire and no airborne fighters on combat air patrol. The Japanese soon realized that these solitary sentinels had limited ability to defend themselves. Little of the savaging of these lonely pickets was recorded by ship's photographers or news reel cameramen. But a sense of the conflict is apparent in the following photos of the battered survivors.

The small ships were also the first to feel the deadly power of the Baka bomb, Japan's wonder weapon. Many were shot down enroute or launched prematurely by their mother planes. But a few did get through, and the first one was successfully piloted into the *Mannert L. Abele* DD-733 on 12 April 1945. The ship had already taken a fatal blow from a Kamikaze when the Baka, piloted, according to Japanese sources by Sublieutenant Saburo Dohi, came hurtling across the water at near 500 mph. Dohi's mother-ship, a Betty twin-engine bomber witnessed the engagement from a distance and returned to report that their Oka had hit a battleship. Casualties on destroyer *Mennert L. Abele* were 6 killed, 73 missing and 35 wounded. According to naval archives only two sinkings were credited to Bakas: *Mennert L. Abele* and a landing craft, LCS(L)-33.

Those seamen who witnessed the rare Baka bomb attacks were in awe of the weapon. Because of its small size and high speed, prospects of shooting one down were very poor.

Japanese aircraft of virtually every type were employed in suicide attacks. There were even a few sorties employing biplane trainers, doubtless with cadet pilots at the controls. Obsolete aircraft, long absent from the more distant battle fronts, were also utilized, such aircraft being as deadly in a ship crashing role as a modern fighter. Ground troops on Ie Shima, adjacent to Okinawa, witnessed many of these lone attacks by dedicated pilots in relics of the 1930s. Capt. Art Nash, with the 318th Fighter Group, provides this eye witness account of a fixed undercarriage Nate's attack over the anchorage:

"It was getting darker and one last fighter flew almost directly overhead. It had an open canopy and I could see the pilot plainly. He had a long white scarf around his neck, and four or five feet of it trailed out in the slipstream. I thought, 'What courage,' and started firing at him with my Garand. Hundreds of others were firing at him too. He was hit hard, nosed down, and rammed a small ship that had been beached and burned out the night before. Our tent was riddled by others firing at the attacker."

The crescendo of conventional and suicide attacks on the fleet around the Ryukyus began late in March 1945 and reached a climax in late May but tapered off about June 21st as U.S. forces finally defeated the last Japanese holdouts. Apart from the terrible casualties on both sides in the battle for the island, Japanese air attacks had extracted the loss of some 36 ships and severe damage to another 360, killing over 5,000 sailors. It is estimated that the Japanese suffered the loss of some 3,000 airplanes and crews, including near 1,800 Kamikazes in the Okinawa campaign.

Sporadic air operations against the Allied fleet, both conventional and suicide, continued until a final flurry in late July 1945 then tapered off. With Okinawa lost the Japanese awaited the inevitable invasion of the Home Islands. Some 12,000 remaining aircraft of all types were camouflaged or hidden in places distant from airfields, husbanded for the final furious Kamikaze onslaught on the invasion fleet. Both Allied ground troops and the men manning the ships feared that confrontation, knowing that no matter how many attackers were shot downed by flak and fighters, some of the Kamikazes would get through. For both combatants that final battle would be one of inordinate savagery. The dropping of two atomic bombs on August 6th and 9th, 1945 precluded that final assault on the Allied fleet as well as an invasion that no doubt would have caused unprecedented casualties on both sides.

Iwo Jima was invaded on 19 Feb 1945. *Saratoga* CV-3, the oldest carrier in the fleet, was one of the units providing air support for the Marines. Late in the day on 21 Feb a flight of Japanese Zekes, student pilots except for their leader, approached the task force and seemed to concentrate on *Saratoga*. No less than six planes attempted to crash on "Sara" within three minutes.. The first two hit the water and bounced into her starboard side. The third hit at the anchor windlass near the bow, while the fourth was mercifully splashed by flak. The fifth struck the flight deck at the port catapult (see preceding page where one Hellcat burns while two others are preparing to be launched). A sixth Zeke, in flames from AA hits, struck the crane on the starboard side. The fires forward (above) were the most damaging, eventually "cooking" the Hellcats preparing to be launched. In the final scene (below) the fires are out and *Saratoga's* crew surveys the damage. With a casualty list of 123 dead and 192 wounded, the venerable carrier was out of the war. (NARS)

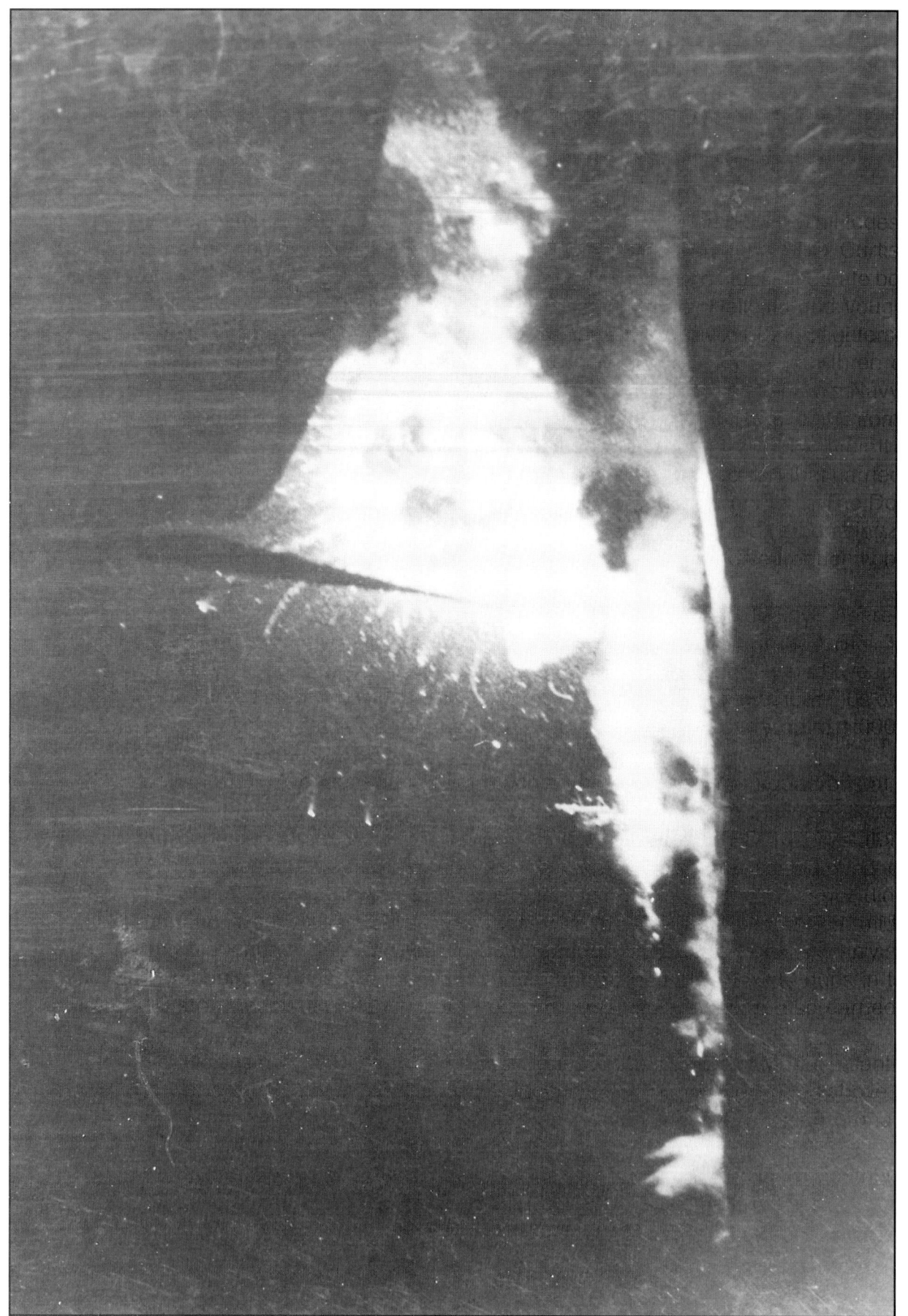

Not long after the attack on *Saratoga*, in a darkening sky, several additional enemy planes attacked the task force off Iwo Jima. One crashed the *Bismarck Sea* CVE-95 abreast the aft elevators causing it to drop to the hangar deck. Gasoline fires were ignited and within minutes the ship was a raging inferno. There being no hope of controlling the fires, her crew abandoned ship. 218 officers and enlisted men of *Bismarck Sea* were lost. (NARS)

Aircraft carriers were always primary targets for both sides in the long Pacific naval war. However, for fledgling Kamikaze pilots of limited skill, but unlimited determination, they were irresistible targets. Shown here is the new *Essex* class *Hornet* CV-12. Her namesake, the CV-8, was lost to Japanese attackers in Oct 1942. *Essex* class fast carriers were the Navy's largest, 855 feet in length and 93 feet wide. The CV-12 was never hit by a Kamikaze. (USN)

Ulithi Atoll in the Western Carolines had become a major Allied fleet anchorage. By March 1945 it was 1,000 miles behind the front lines and thought to be nearly immune from Japanese attack. Japanese reconnaissance had, however, shown Ulithi to be jammed with ships in early March. In a desperate attempt to blunt the next strike by the fast carrier task forces, a Special Attack Unit was dispatched from Kyushu on 11 Mar 1945. It consisted of 24 Mitsubishi Ki-67 Frances twin-engine bombers led by long range flying boats. The overall distance was 1,360 miles, precluding any return. One by one the Frances aircraft fell out of formation due to engine trouble. By the time they reached Yap, fuel shortages caused several more to abort. Only two reached Ulithi on a pitch black night. One crashed on the airstrip damaging several planes. The lone survivor executed well, flying his plane into carrier Randolph CV-15 almost amidships at deck level. The ensuing explosions and fires raged for over six hours (see flight deck above) causing 34 dead and 125 wounded. On the following page damage control personnel can be seen trying to snuff out fires deep in the carrier's bowels. In 25 days Randolph had completed repairs and rejoined the war. (NARS)

A Judy came desperately close to *Essex* CV-9 on 19 Mar 45 before AA gunners tore off a wingtip and deflected the enemy plane to a watery crash. (NARS)

A Japanese attacker is hit near the fleet off the coast of Kyushu. His flaming trail across the sky is watched by tense crew members of the *San Jacinto* CVL-30 who are at battle stations. (NARS)

72

The last land battle of the Pacific war was staged when the U.S. invaded the island of Okinawa in the Ryukyu chain just 300 miles from Japan. D-Day was 1 Apr 1945. The Japanese hurled both conventional air squadrons and suicide units at the Allied fleet with unrelenting fury. First to suffer was the carrier *Franklin*, CV-13. While off the coast of Kyushu, early on 19 Mar 1945, the *Franklin* had already launched a strike of 45 aircraft. A second strike of 31 planes were waiting their turn, loaded with gasoline and ordnance, some with props turning. Suddenly, a lone, undetected Japanese bomber plummeted out of the overcast and dropped two bombs squarely on the flight deck's massed aircraft. Fuel tanks, .50 cal rounds, bombs and rockets and some ready ammunition near flak batteries began to "cook off", adding to the carnage (above). See following pages for more on the *Franklin* saga. (NARS)

Cruiser *Santa Fe* (foreground) CL-60 quickly closed with *Franklin* to render assistance and help fight fires, then *Pittsburgh CA-72* got a tow line aboard. (NARS)

An aft five inch gun mount on *Franklin* began to burn, but was extinguished by fire hoses from *Santa Fe.* (NARS)

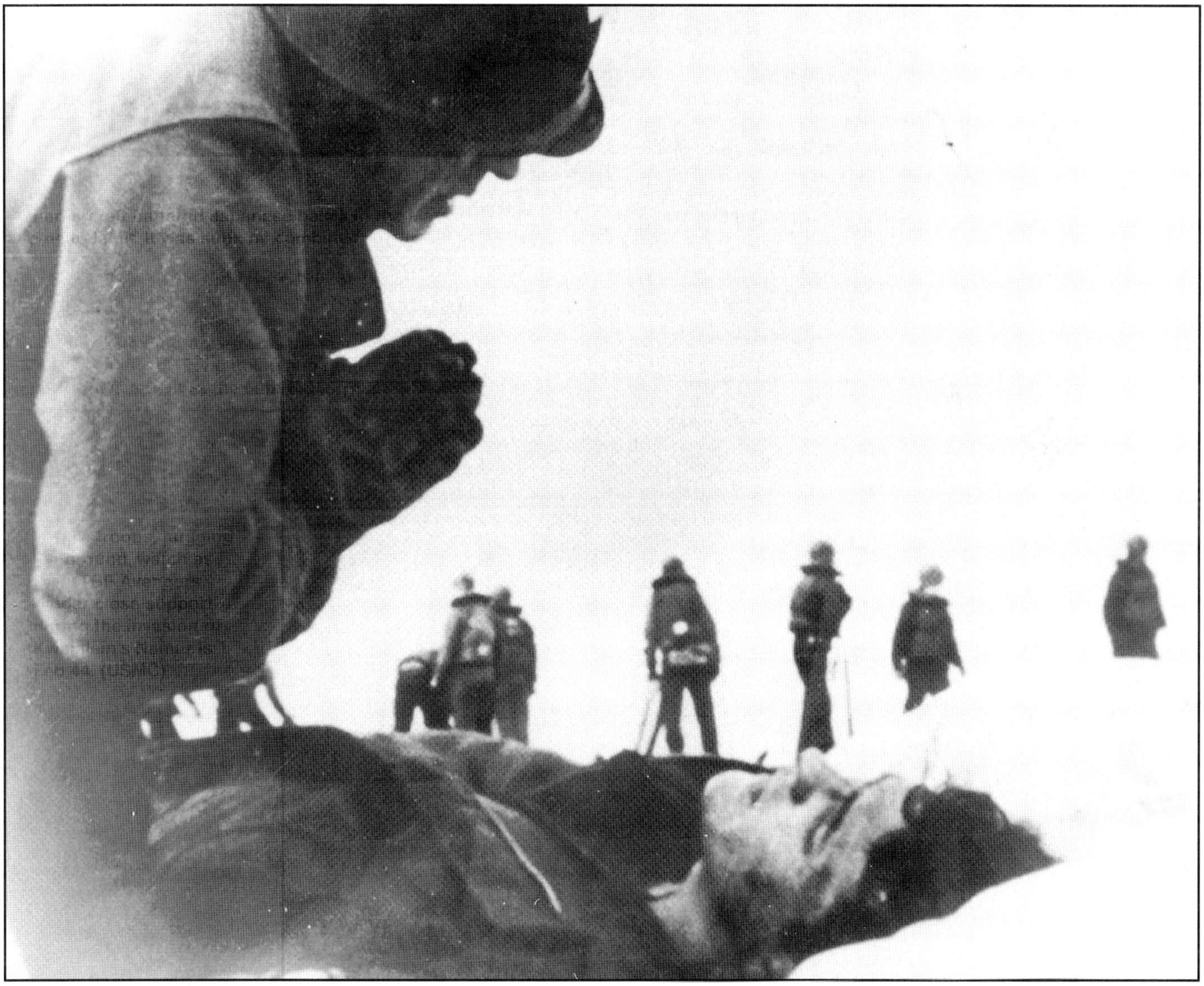

By mid-afternoon *Franklin*'s gallant crew with the assistance of other ships, had gotten the fires under control and managed to get up power. Acts of bravery among the crew were common, but none outdid Chaplain Joseph O'Callahan, (above in one of the war's most famous photos) who though wounded, rescued men trapped on lower decks, tended the injured, gave succor to the dying and fought fires. He was later awarded the Medal of Honor. *Franklin* was out of the war but, with a partial crew, made it home to Pearl Harbor and then to the States. Her casualties in this incident were an astonishing 801 killed or missing and 265 wounded. In a previous Kamikaze encounter and counting air operations casualties *Franklin* lost a total of 921 in the war. (NARS)

Amid a hailstorm of AA fire, a Japanese Judy is seen fleeing across the fleet after an unsuccessful bomb run on a carrier near Kyushu on 20 March 1945. (NARS).

The Judy from the previous page, apparently not bent on suicide, leads a seemingly charmed life as it runs the gauntlet of ships' anti-aircraft fire (above) but is finally dispatched in flames (below). (NARS)

20 Mar 1945 off the coast of Kyushu. The destroyer, *Halsey Powell* DD-686, had just finished refueling from carrier *Hancock* when a Zeke dove on the combined target. Quickly casting off and ringing up flank speed the destroyer turned hard left rudder to unteather and separate from the giant carrier. The Zeke narrowly missed the flight deck of *Hancock* but succeeded in crashing on *Halsey Powell's* stern near the 5-inch gun mount (above). With her steering gear damaged in the hard over position she narrowly averted a collision with *Hancock*. *Halsey Powell* survived the attack but lost 12 killed and 29 wounded. (USN)

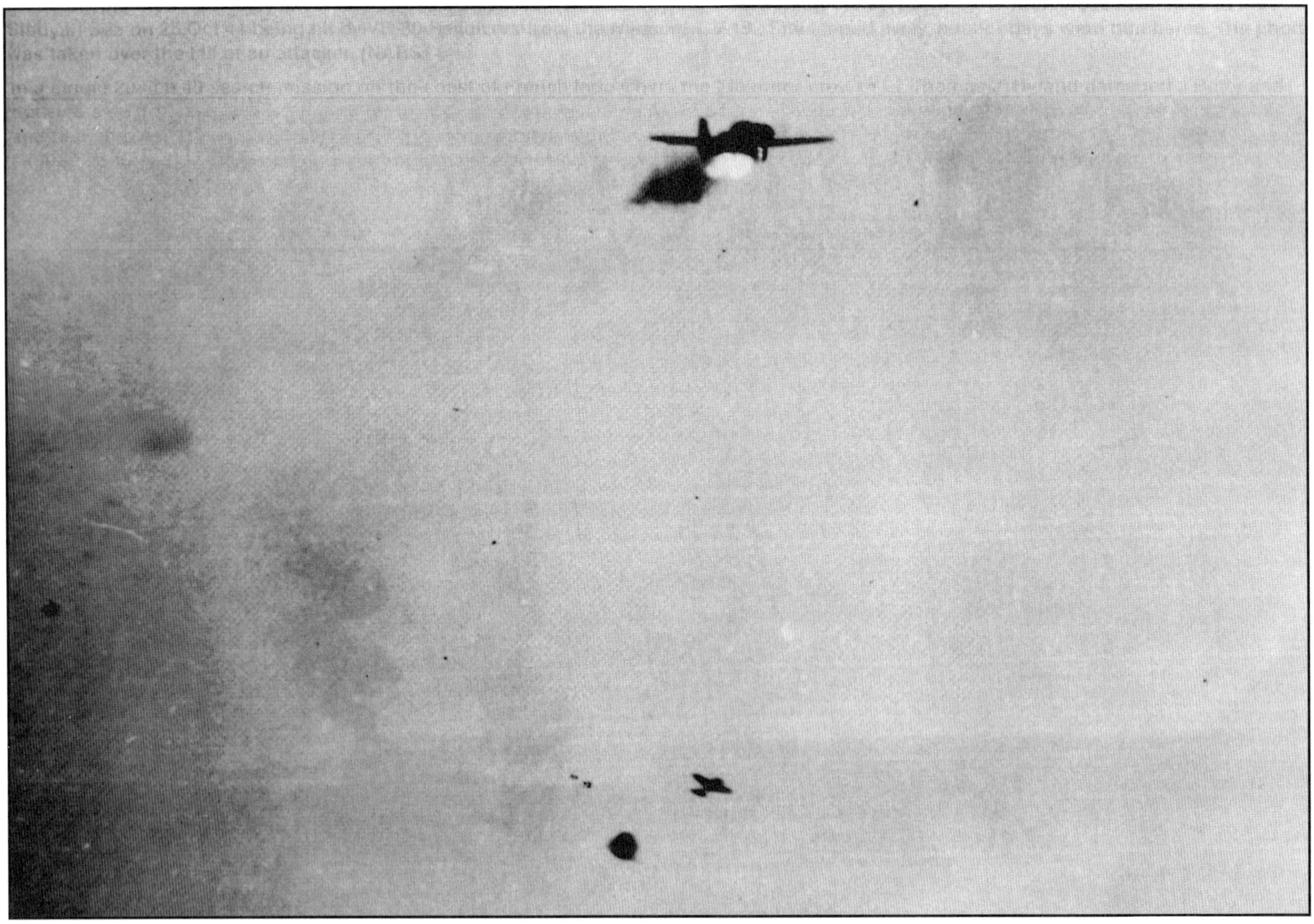

Near Okinawa on 29 Mar 45 a Judy attacked *Yorktown* CV-10. The defensive fire put up by *Yorktown* and her escorts not only bagged the Judy (above) but also damaged a pursuing F6F Hellcat of VF-9 (below). The Judy crashed and the F6F ditched, its pilot being rescued by a destroyer. (NARS)

78

Okinawa was invaded on 1 Apr 1945. Japanese air attacks against the fleet built to a furious climax on 6 Apr when 28 ships were hit and 6 sunk. *Newcomb* DD-586 (above) beat off five attackers on 6 Apr but two crashed into her inflicting devastating damage above the waterline, killing 40 and wounding 24 of her crew. She is shown here moored in Kerama Retto anchorage several days later as the crew stares in wonderment at the damage and no doubt considers their own brush with death. (NARS)

A Kamikaze crashes on 6 Apr 1945 (above) just off the bow of *San Jacinto* CVL-30, killing one and injuring three. Seconds after the incident (below), crew members rush to aid the casualties and attend the damage. (NARS)

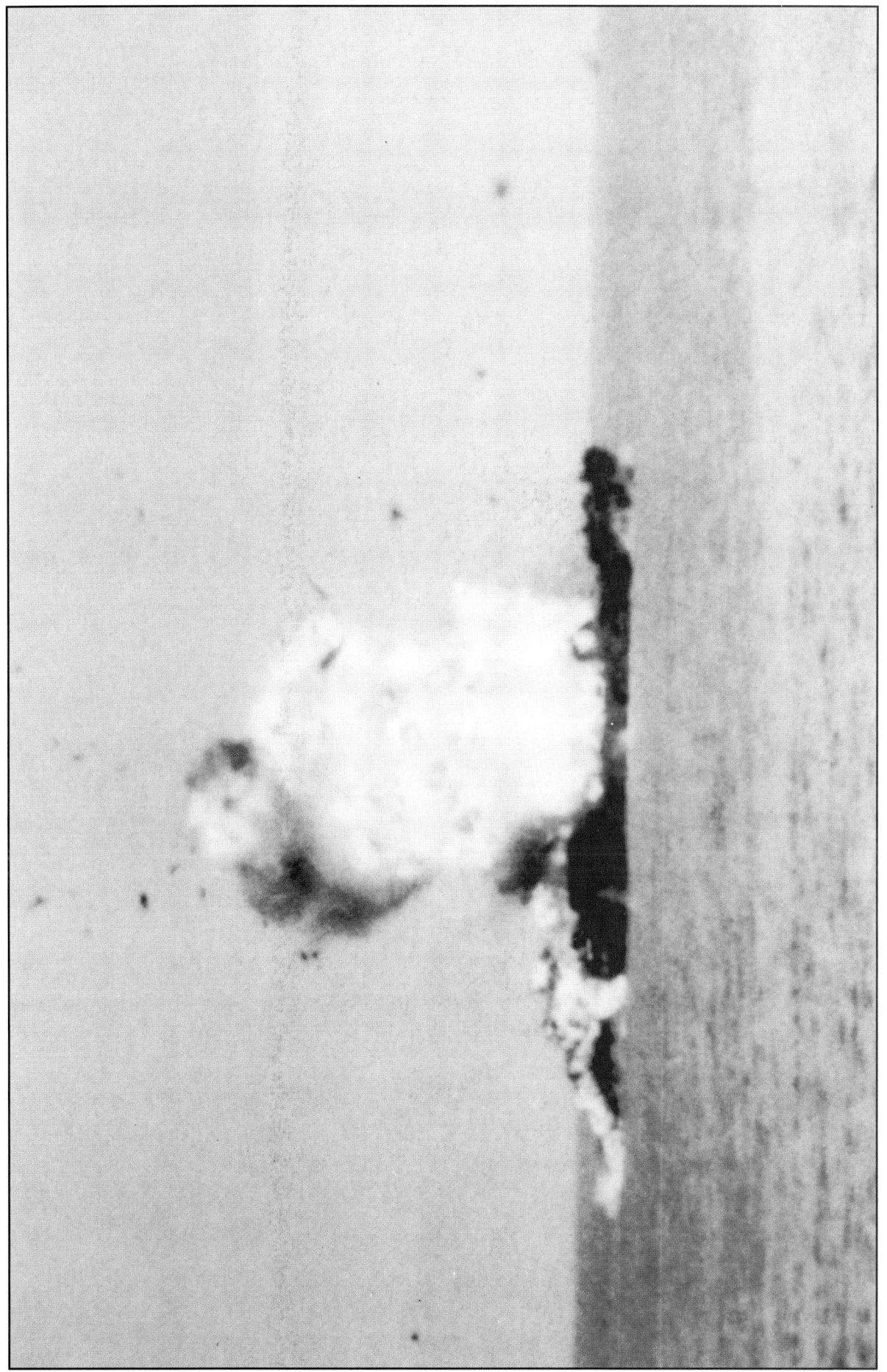

In the devastating Kamikaze attacks of 6 Apr 45 the small ships were generally ignored for the higher profile, naval targets and big transports. One Zeke bound for the invasion fleet was fired at and hit by the batteries of LST-447. The Japanese pilot turned toward the small ship, apparently figuring that she was his only option. LST-447's crew bravely continued to fire until the Zeke hit (above) exploding the cargo of diesel fuel. The crew was forced to abandon the flaming mass within ten minutes. LST-447 lost 5 killed and had 17 wounded, 18 per cent of her complement. (NARS)

Destroyer *Leutze* DD-481 (above) took many casualties on 6 Apr 1945, 7 dead and 34 wounded, from a Kamikaze that hit near her fantail and ended draped across her stern, just aft of the 5 inch gun mount. (NARS)

The near misses were frequent and nearly as harrowing as the hits. Here fighters from the Combat Air Patrols (CAPs) save two ships from disaster. Above: A Val intending to attack *Idaho* BB-42 was disabled by a Grumman Navy Wildcat and fell short of the battleship. Below: Pursued by a pair of Marine Corsairs, a Kamikaze pilot crashes and explodes harmlessly off the port beam of carrier *Sitkoh Bay*, CVE-86. (USN)

While Japanese air units were assaulting the fleet off Okinawa, the Japanese fleet sortied for a climactic final battle led by super battleship *Yamato*. Task Force 58 maneuvered for an attack on *Yamato* and her consorts on 7 Apr 1945. Swarms of Japanese planes were attracted to the carrier strike force and although some 18 were downed by flak and fighters one got through to crash the deck of *Hancock* CV-19. Minutes after the incident (above) she appeared to be helplessly engulfed in flames. But heroic efforts by damage control parties (following page) brought the fires under control. (See succeeding pages for more of the *Hancock*.) (NARS)

After attending to her many casualties (left) and repairing her deck (below) *Hancock* was back in the fight. She lost 72 killed and 82 wounded. (NARS)

A Japanese Kamikaze pilot misses *Sangamon* CVE-26 by the narrowest of margins (right) on 8 Apr 45. (NARS)

11 Apr 1945. Another Japanese Kamikaze is deflected by the combined fire of ships' AA. (below) The ugly black puffs are air bursts of large caliber guns, each puff marking the spot where a storm of shrapnel fills the air. The Japanese aircraft crashed off the port side of *Pasadena* CL-65 as seen from *Essex*. (NARS)

A Japanese Zero can be seen speeding over the wave tops, on 11 Apr 1945 at *Missouri* BB-63 (preceding page), having escaped the concentrated AA fire of the fleet. Now it is too close and too low for the battleship's gunners to depress many of their weapons. The Zero, a Hamp version, is next pictured (above) just before striking the hull about three feet below main deck level. Although airplane parts and fragments of the pilot were scattered all over the ship's starboard side, there was remarkably little damage and no serious casualties to *Missouri*. (NARS)

The Yokosuka Model 11 Oka (Cherry Blossom), or "Baka" as the Americans dubbed it, is shown above on Okinawa. Below, a photo taken from the rear with the tail assembly removed, reveals the rockets. Once launched from a mother-ship it could attain 534 mph in level flight, much faster than any Allied fighter of that day. In a dive the Baka achieved well over 600 mph, too fast to lead with anti-aircraft guns. Only a lucky hit could destroy one. Built in two versions, with a 1,300 or 2,600 lb warheads, either had a devastating effect. Most were lost while vulnerably attached to their mother-ships before reaching targets. (Lambert)

A series of gun camera photos by a Navy fighter (unit unk.) shows the attack on a Mitsubishi Betty bomber carrying an Oka or Baka rocket bomb beneath its belly. Both were shot down before the Oka could be launched. In the final photo (below) flames glow from fire started on the Betty. (NARS)

As the Japanese Army Air Force began to get into the Kamikaze business, their Kawanishi Ki-61Hien single-seat fighter (Tony in Allied nomenclature) was seen increasingly by the U.S. Navy. This swift fighter (a captured version shown above), was a match for any combat air patrols over the fleet and many got through to crash on target. (Lambert)

The Nakajima Ki-43 Oscar (below) was the principle Japanese Army fighter for much of World War II. It was extraordinarily maneuverable but lightly armed. (NARS)

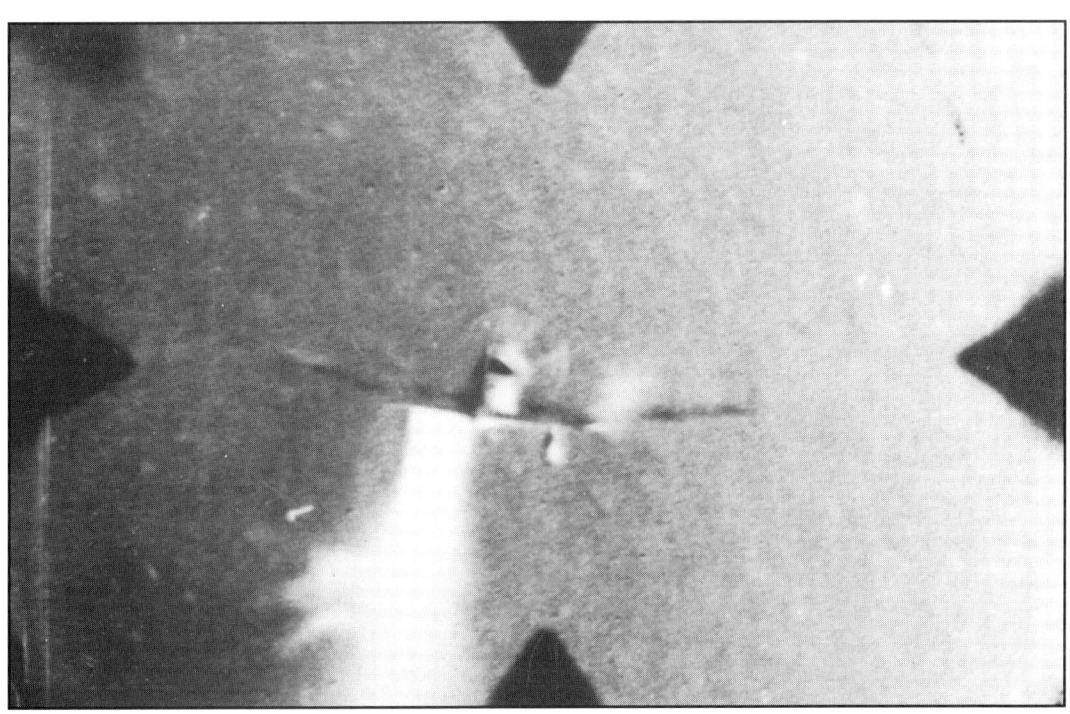

The Nakajima Ki-27 (Nate by Allied designation) was a fighter of the 1930s that went out of production before the U.S. entered the war. It was used as a trainer by the Japanese Army, but toward the close of the war they were employed in suicide attacks. Caught by defending fighters they were easily downed, but even obsolete aircraft that evaded flak and fighters could be deadly weapons against ships in the Kamikaze role. This pair is from the Akeno Fighter School. (Don Thorpe via Jim Lansdale)

Lt. Cdr. James C. Longino, CO of VF-40 flying F6F Hellcats from *Suwanee*, downed a pair of ancient Japanese Sonias on 13 Apr 1945 near Okinawa as shown in this gun camera clip. Obsolete before the start of the Pacific war, the Japanese used these fixed gear, open cockpit aircraft for Army obser- vation and as trainers, but found them suitable instruments for a cadet bent on self destruction. (NARS)

Little *Lindsey* DM-32 survived the Kamikaze crashes of two Val dive-bombers, one of which took off most of the destroyer-mine layer's bow. Lindsey lost 50 of her crew and had another 57 wounded in this 12 Apr 1945 action. She is at anchor here off Okinawa. (NARS)

Destroyer *Sigsbee* DD-502 on picket duty near Task Force 58, was put out of the fight by a Kamikaze that crashed her stern on 14 Apr 1945. The suicide plane sheared off the last 40 feet of *Sigsbee*. She lost 22 killed and 74 wounded, and had to be towed to Guam for repairs. (NARS)

Battleship *Missouri* was hit by another Kamikaze on 16 Apr 45, again without serious casualties. The enemy fighter hit the giant ship a glancing blow leaving a machine gun dangling from a 40mm battery. (NARS)

A Zeke dives through the AA fire of carrier *Hornet* CV-12 to be splashed on 16 Apr near the Ryukyus. (NARS)

On 16 Apr 45 a Japanese Kate charges through a veritable curtain of anti-aircraft fire from many ships toward *New Mexico* BB-35, coming directly at the camera. Shell bursts from heavy batteries blacken the skies above and create dark geysers while rapid fire 20 and 40mm cannons send up waterspouts in the foreground. *New Mexico* survived the engagement but the brave Japanese pilot did not. (NARS)

Left: Belly view of a Japanese Frances hit by AA and aflame at both engines near battleship *Wisconsin* BB-64 in waters near the Ryukyu Islands. (NARS)

Standing off Okinawa on 16 Apr 1945 *Intrepid* CV-11became a target for two Kamikazes. One crashed close aboard but the second plunged into her stern flight deck causing extensive damage, killing 10, injuring 87 and knocking *Intrepid* out of the war. Here damage control parties attempt to quench the fires below decks. This was the fourth time that *Intrepid* had been hit by suicide attackers. (NARS)

While riding at anchor on 4 May 1945, cruiser *Birmingham* CL-62 took a hit by a Japanese Army Nakajima Ki-42 Oscar on the main deck close to the No. 2 5-inch turret (above). The bomb it was carrying passed through the ship's sick bay killing patients and medical staff. *Birmingham* lost 51 killed and had 81 wounded. (NARS)

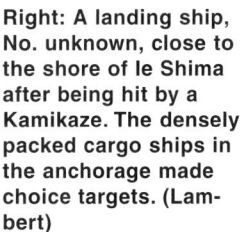

Right: A landing ship, No. unknown, close to the shore of Ie Shima after being hit by a Kamikaze. The densely packed cargo ships in the anchorage made choice targets. (Lambert)

Operating off the Ryukyus on 29 Apr 45, *Hazelwood* DD-531 was assisting her battle damaged sister ship, *Haggard* DD-555, into the Kerama Retto Anchorage when two Kamikazes attacked the new target. *Hazelwood*'s AA batteries splashed the first close alongside, but the second Japanese aircraft crashed her on the port side at the superstructure main deck level. Her captain and 45 others perished and 26 were wounded. Note her main mast toppled over the side. (NARS)

Aaron Ward DM-34, a mine layer converted from a destroyer, was performing radar picket duty some 70 miles southwest of Okinawa on 3 May 45. For no apparent reason she was singled out by a host of Formosa based Japanese Army and Navy aircraft of all types. *Aaron Ward* fought nine separate attackers, shooting down four. However, five either crashed the ship or hit close alongside, all inflicting damage of varying degrees. In the end the gallant little ship was afloat but dead in the water without steering. Towed into Kerama Retto anchorage, she had casualties of 45 dead and 49 wounded. (NARS)

Escort carrier *Sangamon* had a second brush with death in the form of a Kamikaze on 11 May 1945 as a Kawasaki Ki-61 Tony (above) crashed alongside near dusk. That was the end of *Sangamon's* luck. A short time later a twin-engine Kawasaki Ki-45 Nick dove out of darkening clouds and struck the center of the flight deck, causing enormous damage that put the carrier out of the war. She lost 21 members of her crew in the attack. (USN)

Light cruiser *Vicksburg* CL-86 and other ships of the fleet down this Japanese attacker and capture his death dive and plunge into the ocean off Japan. (NARS)

11 May 1945 was a day of disaster for *Bunker Hill* CV-17. About 10:40 AM with no radar warning, a Zeke was seen diving on the carrier. The Japanese plane, carrying a 500 lb. bomb hit on the after flight deck. Just as crew members were recovering from the shock of that strike, a Judy was seen approaching from the stern. This second suicide bomber hit the flight deck just aft of the island superstructure. The Judy also carried a bomb that penetrated to lower decks before exploding (above). After hours of gallant fire fighting and damage control *Bunker Hill's* crew, with assistance from other ships (*Wilkes-Barre* CL-130 seen left, below) suppressed the fires, got underway and departed the battle area. *Bunker Hill* had lost 396 dead or missing and had 264 wounded. The extent of damage was adjudged second only to that of *Franklin*. (NARS)

During the approach to Okinawa and the initial landings, CAP for the fleet was provided by carrier based Hellcats, Wildcats and Corsairs. Starting April 7 Marine Air Groups 31, 33, and 22 landed at Yontan and Kadena airfields and began to provide close ground support as well as fighter cover for the fleet. Shown above is a Chance Vought F4U-1D Corsair (factory fresh). The first Army fighters to arrive and lend a hand were Republic P-47N Thunderbolts of the 318th Ftr. Grp in May flying from Ie Shima. Below is a Thunderbolt from the 333rd Sq, 318th. (Lambert)

A pair of aces who helped protect the Okinawa invasion armada: 1st Lt. John W. Ruhsam (above), of VMF-323, is shown on his Corsair adorned with six aerial "kill" flags. He scored his first victory on 12 Apr 45, bagged 4 Vals on 5 May, and ended the war with a total of 7 victories. (USMC via NARS)

Right: Capt. Judge E. Wolfe, 333rd Ftr. Sq. who scored a total of seven victories during the period 28 May and 10 Jun 45, all between Kyushu and Okinawa. These claims and two previous kills over Iwo Jima adorn his P-47N. (Lambert)

This remarkable sequence, taken through the rigging of *Enterprise* , shows the approach of a Zeke on 14 May 1945, (above) as tracers reach out from the ship's gunners. The pilot, Lt. Tomai Kai, flying from a Kyushu airbase, rolls his plane upside down at the last instant (left). With a 550 lb. bomb slung below the fuselage, he plunges toward the deck of *Enterprise. (Bill Balden)*

The instant result of the crash on *Enterprise*, as viewed from an escorting ship, was an explosion that blew the forward elevator nearly 1,000 feet in the air. Casualties were 14 dead and 68 wounded. Gallant *Enterprise* had been in the war from the first day, but after this attack she was out of the fight for good. (John MacGlashing)

Natoma Bay CVE-62 narrowly escaped a Japanese suicide plane on 6 Jun 45. The Kamikaze fell alongside but strafed the flight deck on his approach setting fire to an FM-2 Wildcat. The fires were quickly extinguished and there were no casualties. (NARS)

William D. Porter DD-686 was on picket duty 35 miles north of Okinawa on 10 Jun 45. The Kamakaze's had been infrequent, but suddenly a Val dove on *Porter* from a low cloud layer. The Japanese pilot narrowly missed the ship but his bomb detonated under-water, tearing open seams in the after engine room and she sank by the stern. Here LCS-122 draws close to rescue *Porter's* crew, which suffered injuries but no deaths. The very next day LCS-122 was hit by a Val suffering 11 dead and many wounded, but she retired under her own power. (NARS)

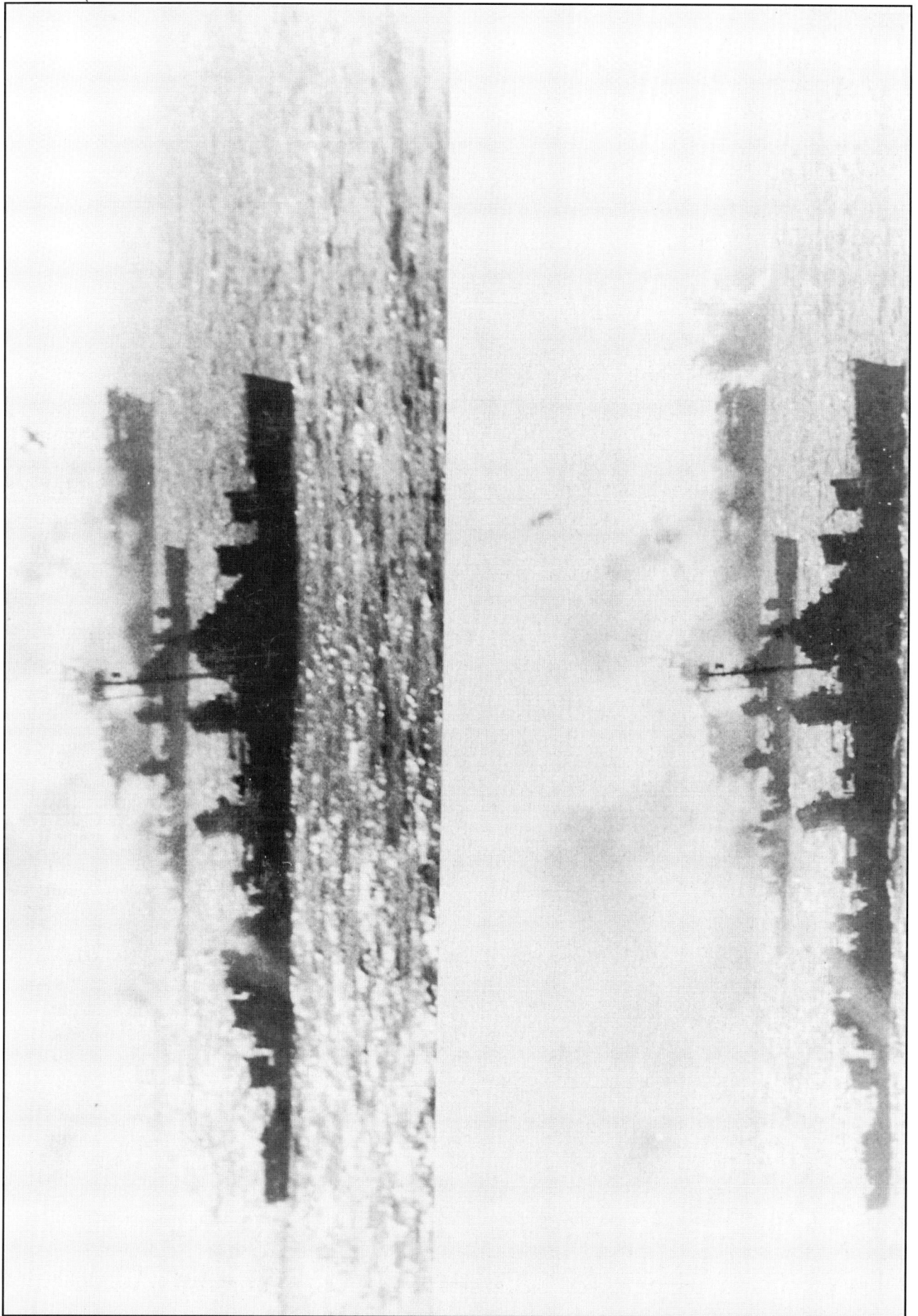

In this sequence a Japanese Aicha B7A Grace torpedo bomber, being employed as a Kamikaze, dives toward the distant aircraft carrier *Wasp* CV-18, landing in the water off the starboard bow. It was 9 Aug 1945 off the coast of Japan. (NARS)

The last victim of the last Kamikaze: Attack transport *La Grange* APA-124 (above) was hit off Okinawa on 13 Aug 45, the eve of VJ day. The converted Liberty Ship made a huge target. Her crew examines the point of impact (below). (NARS)